The River, the Kettle And the Bird

A TORAH GUIDE TO SUCCESSFUL MARRIAGE

by

AHARON FELDMAN

based on a transcription by Shimon Brodie of the author's lectures

C S B PUBLICATIONS

ISBN No. 0-87306-440-2

8

Distributed by:
Philip Feldheim Inc.
200 Airport Executive Park
Spring Valley, NY 10977/(914) 356-2282
                        (800) 237-7149

Available in Israel from:
C S B Publications c/o Brodie
Rechov Menachem Mayshiv 4, Jerusalem

Printed In Israel

בן יכבד אב

In Gratitude

To my beloved parents

RABBI AND MRS. JOSEPH H. FELDMAN

אאמו״ר מוהר״ר הרב הגאון יוסף פלדמן ורעיתו שליט״א

whose life-long love, devotion and sacrifice for each other

are an embodiment of the ideas of this book

עוד ינובון בשיבה דשנים דשנים ורעננים יהיו

הסכמה

LETTER OF APPROBATION
by HaRav HaGaon Jacob I. Ruderman זצוק״ל
Late Rosh Hayeshivah, Ner Israel Rabbinical College
Baltimore, Md.

מכבוד מורי ורבי פאר הדור הגאון הגדול

יעקב יצחק הלוי רודרמן זצוק״ל

לא מצא הקב״ה כלי מחזיק ברכה לישראל אלא השלום

(סוף עוקצין)

אמר רב חנן שלש שלומות הן נהר צפור וקדרה

(ברכות נו ב׳)

TABLE OF CONTENTS

PREFACE

A few years ago I gave a series of weekly lectures at a Yeshiva in Jerusalem on the topic of *Shalom Bayis* (marital peace). The talks were geared for men in their first year or two of married life and were intended to provide a Torah-based approach to married life. They explored the reasons for marital conflict and offered practical advice on how to eliminate them. I was quite surprised to discover that this quickly became the most popular class I had ever given. The class attracted young people from a wide variety of backgrounds and from varied walks of life. Some of these came because they had marital difficulties, but most who attended did so not because they had trouble with their marriages, but simply because they felt a critical need to hear more about one of the most vital areas of their lives — and one of the least discussed.

Before his wedding every Torah-observant man undergoes a course of study on the halachic aspects of marriage; few, however, are given a realistic view of how to act and what to expect after marriage. The most that they will hear on this subject will be some lofty platitudes about: how marriage is man's completion as a human being, how it brings sanctity to life if used properly, how a Jewish home must become a bastion of Torah learning and *chessed* (lovingkindness). These are all truisms but unfortunately the most critical factor of a successful marriage is omitted: that to realize these truths one has to learn how to get along with his spouse — a process which entails constant effort in improving one's character.

Not only was the advice offered by the lectures in itself beneficial, but the very fact that the problem was being discussed contributed to its solution. *Shalom Bayis* concerns an intimate part of one's life. Dissension between man and wife usually takes place where there are no witnesses; embarrassment makes them hide any trace of it; and the fact that domestic strife is common is a very well-kept secret. Because of this, couples with marital problems experience a sense of extreme personal failure, which makes them feel too hopeless and ashamed to seek help. A tremendous sense of relief, therefore, accompanies the discovery that the problem is ubiquitous, that the situations which cause discord are quite standard — enough that they can be described by an outsider. The relief and the newly gained sense of perspective create an impetus to start solving the problems.

All of this crystallized for me the importance of recording the content of the lectures in book form. After many revisions the substance of these talks is now thoroughly recast for presentation in book form. I pray that it will prove equally useful to a much wider audience of Jewish couples, those about to be married as well as those newly — and "oldly" —wed.

The Perspective of This Book

The perspective on marriage offered in this book is that which emerges from the Torah and its commentaries. Ultimately, this is a perspective not only on marriage but on life itself. The Torah sees man as a creation of God who is given the opportunity to achieve happiness by drawing himself closer to Him. This is done by channelling, as well as controlling, man's selfish interests for power and pleasure, and striving instead for spiritual growth. Although every human drive has its place in the service of God, the Torah teaches that making gratification the goal of life causes the disintegration of both man and society. Human success can only be ensured if man will avoid self-centeredness and learn to control those selfish drives which, by definition, militate against spiritual growth.

The truths which the Torah teaches are, ultimately, not a product of human intelligence. They are, rather, based on a Divinely imparted teaching based on the knowledge of the mysteries of creation and the secrets of the structure of the human psyche. These are truths deriving from the very formulae of existence, which only God himself could know. The laws of the Torah are designed to keep man in tune with these formulae and thereby nourish the deepest needs of his being. Because of this, they are the best path to true human success and happiness. This explains why those who have kept its ways have, for thousands of years in thousands of different environments, created the most successful societies on the face of earth.

This Torah outlook often clashes strongly with that of much of the modern secular world. I refer to that outlook which reduces man to an accident of evolution whose life lacks intrinsic meaning and purpose, and which favors filling the vacuum of life with a maximum of emotional and sensual gratification. By these guidelines, the very achievements which this sort of secular outlook would consider success are those which a Torah Jew would brand failure.

It is the premise of this book that only through the Torah perspective can complete marital happiness ever be achieved. It is based on the thesis that the creation of domestic happiness is accomplished through an awareness of one's goals in life, through self-control, and through efforts toward character improvement. Obviously, then, one should not look in this book for instant solutions and magic answers, for changes in one's attitudes and responses towards life cannot be expected immediately. Likewise, a cursory, one-time reading of this book will achieve little. Only after continued study and internalization of its principles will one be able to deal with, and overcome, the major obstacles to a happy marriage.

Another note should be made on the book's perspective: Partly because of the nature of the lectures which were its origins, many parts of the book are written from a man's, and not a woman's, viewpoint. I tried to adjust the original content of these parts for use by women as well, but had to abandon the attempt when I found this impossible. Man and woman view marriage from different perspectives; also, each has different emotional needs and weaknesses with which he or she must deal. It is therefore not always possible to write for both perspectives simultaneously. However, although these sections were written from a man's viewpoint, women will nevertheless gain much by reading them since this will give them invaluable insight into the institution of marriage.

ACKNOWLEDGMENTS

Anyone who is aided by this book owes a debt of gratitude to Rabbi Shimon Brodie, a respected Torah scholar and *kollel* member living in Jerusalem, without whom it would have never been written. His notes of the lectures, which he attended faithfully and (with the help of his father, Dr. David Brodie) transcribed into an excellent typewritten adaptation, formed the basis of the book; and it was he who stood by my side with assistance and encouragement until the book was completed. I therefore hereby express my deepest thanks to him for his untiring and devoted efforts. May he be blessed with all the blessings promised by the Torah to one who occupies himself selflessly with benefitting the general community (*zikuy harabim*).

I also express my gratitude to the following people for the important roles they played in the publication of this book:

To my brother, Rabbi Emanuel Feldman, for bringing to bear on the manuscript his outstanding skills as a noted writer and his vast experience as the spiritual leader of Orthodox Jewry in Atlanta, Georgia, for thirty-five years. Nearly all of his many suggestions were incorporated into the final version.

To Dr. Uri Cheskin, for his invaluable editorial assistance which contributed immeasurably to the literary quality of this book.

To the many friends and students, especially to Moshe Isser Kravitz, Jonathan Rosenblum, and Moshe Efros, who took time to read the manuscript and offer important suggestions.

To those who unselfishly aided me in the the most vital aspects of producing the manuscript and publishing the book, in particular to my former students, Daniel Spekman and Shimon Garrel.

To Dr. Jeffery Feigenbaum, a scientist engaged in neurological experimentation, for his assistance in researching parts of Chapter Six.

To Yaakov Feldheim, of Feldheim Publishers, Ltd. whose gracious advice was extremely valuable in the final production stages of the book.

May they all be blessed, *mida kenegged mida,* with finding peace and fulfillment in their own lives.

Last, but most important, an inadequate expression of gratitude to the one person without whom my life would be without joy, without blessing, and without Torah, and, certainly, without whom the writing of this book — or for that matter anything else useful in my life — could never have been accomplished: my wife, Lea Feldman.

In beginning this book, I offer a fervent prayer, using the words of the Tanna, R. Yonasan ben Uziel, that this book be written "not for my honor and not for the honor of my father's household, but for Your honor, so that there be no more controversy in Israel." May this book make some modest contribution towards investing Jewish homes and marriages with the Torah values of family peace and love. May He who makes peace in His celestial heights make peace among us and upon all of Israel.

A.F.
Jerusalem,
11 Shevat, 5747

1

THE NAME OF THIS BOOK

The name of this book is taken from a passage in the Talmud which says that one who dreams of a river, a kettle, or a bird can look forward to peace.[1]

These are three symbols of peace because they represent three possible levels of human peaceful relationships. By extension, they are also a description of the stages of development of a successful marriage and therefore serve well as the framework for the ideas of this book.

In its lowest form peace means the absence of conflict, or peace in a purely negative sense. This state exists when two people or groups of people maintain contact with each other to the extent that this serves each of their interests. Although there is an active relationship between them, each member to this sort of peace remains a separate and discrete unit. The symbol for this type of peace is a river. A river is the classic vehicle of commerce between two cities. As such, it represents a state of communication which exists between two separate entities connected only by their mutual benefit.

There is a second degree of peace. This exists where two people or groups of people join together to reach a common goal which neither alone would be able to achieve. For example, individuals band together to build skyscrapers; corporations form monopolies to increase their competitiveness; nations join in mutual defense pacts. None of these could be performed by each participant alone; only the joint efforts of all parties working together achieve the desired aims. This is not mere co-existence. This represents a type of peace which is dynamic, resulting in the achievement of an objective which could not have been reached if not for the peace.

This type of peace is symbolized by a kettle. A kettle is designed to prepare food by utilizing the combined talents of water and fire. Water alone would ruin the food through soaking. Fire alone would burn it. But through the mediatory effect of the kettle, an environment proper for cooking is created. The kettle harnesses the talent of water to retain heat and the talent of fire to produce it to create an edible product. The kettle has thus made possible a productive peace between fire and water.

The third and final level of peace is the peace of the bird. A bird has two disparate talents: the ability to survive on earth as well as to fly in the heavens. These talents are not separate skills which exist side by side. Rather, they are details of a single organism which operates in these two realms. The way the bird walks on earth is affected by the way it is designed to fly. Conversely, the way it flies the heavens is affected by the way it is intended to walk the earth. It is simultaneously both an earthbound and airborne being. A bird, therefore, represents an embodiment of a peace where two natures and two entities have merged into one unit. The two parties to this sort of peace not only work together but in doing so have merged into one unit. For example, the fifty states of the United States are not individual entities, but have submerged their individual identities into the common unit to which they belong.

Each of these three levels of peace can exist in a marriage, each level reflecting the degree to which the peace between man and wife has become internalized.

The simplest level of marriage is the peace of the river. Each marriage partner is prepared to fulfil his duties and obligations to his spouse faithfully, but each lives his own separate and individual life. They have learned to avoid disagreements and to live together peacefully, but although they do not quarrel, there is little emotional attachment present.

The second level, the peace of the kettle, exists in a marriage in which goals are set which each partner would be unable to achieve separately. As they work together towards these goals, and each senses how he could not function without the contributions of the other, an emotional bond based on mutual dependency begins to form between them. Unlike the peace of the first level, this peace becomes internalized.

Generally, the very nature of married life leads to this type of peace. Neither of the couple can be both bread-winner and household manager; neither can serve both as father and as mother; each needs the other to create a functioning household. Running a home and rearing a family creates a mutual dependency — and bond — between man and wife. However, the emotion which binds them is of the sort described in the Mishna in *Avos*,[2] a "love dependent upon a cause." The marriage is, for the most part, a utilitarian vehicle for achieving their goals. When these goals no longer exist there is nothing left to bind them.

The well-known "empty nest" divorces of middle-aged couples occur in marriages which have never gone beyond this kettle stage of peace. At a time of life when physical attraction weakens, when the children have grown and left home — especially when the wife no longer needs her husband to support her — there is no longer a reason for the couple to stay together. Their mutual goals have disappeared. As the Mishna cited above regarding love dependent upon a cause concludes: "When the cause is gone, the love is gone as well."

The third and highest level of peace in marriage is peace which has become completely internalized. This is the peace which stems from a deep sense of identity which each marriage partner feels for the other. The relationship has become so vital and meaningful that neither of them conceives of himself as a separate entity. An emotional bond has been created between them which has gone beyond the feeling of mutual dependency or awareness of benefits received. Each is as keenly sensitive to the other's needs as if they were his own. Each is as happy to give to the other as he is to receive from him. There is no separate sensation of "I"; there is only "we." A selfless love exists between them which transcends all reason.

This is the stage of marriage described by the Prophet Malachi as: "והיא חברתך ואשת בריתך" — "For she is your comrade and the wife of your covenant."[3] "The wife of your covenant" is a perfect description of this stage. For "covenant" in Hebrew is ברית, which stems from the word בריאה/creation. The two members to a covenant have become part of a new creation, a new entity. Marriage as covenant is therefore marriage in its ultimate perfection. It is the peace of the bird — the sum of whose parts equals one.

How does one move towards this ultimate stage of marriage? The answer is that the peace of the bird depends upon the peace of the kettle, and the peace of the kettle depends upon the peace of the river. This means that a couple can become totally bound to each other (the peace of the bird) only after they have lived and worked together successfully (the peace of the kettle). For only then will they have learned to trust each other, whereas without trust they can never become totally identified with each other. But they can only live and work together successfully if they have learned to get along with each other on an elemental human level (the peace of the river). In the terms used by the Sages, this means that whoever sees a river *and* a kettle *and* a bird in his home will have achieved full and total marital success.

Most marriages founder on the peace of the river: the couple never learn to get along with each other, respectfully and courteously, without annoyance or anger. Since this relationship is the foundation of the success of marriage, much of this book deals with mastering this level. This means confronting the following questions: what is marriage meant to be; what are its obligations; how should man and wife treat each other; how can one learn to recognize the needs of a woman; how can one learn to control anger. When these problems are mastered, man and wife can learn to work peacefully together towards their lives' goals and create a loving relationship. The stage is then set for the ultimate level of marriage: "For she is your comrade and the wife of your covenant."

NOTES TO CHAPTER ONE

1. *Berachos 56b*. Some of the ideas that follow are based on the commentary of the Vilna Gaon in *Beyurey Hagra La-Agados* to *Berachos, ad loc.*
2. *Avos 5, 16.*
3. *Malachi 2:14.*

2

WHY MARRIAGES DON'T WORK

Domestic discord is probably the most widespread form of human misery. It is rare to find a husband and wife who do not quarrel intermittently, if not frequently.

Every argument between a man and wife is extremely damaging, draining the flavor out of life and putting a halt to productive activity. Quarrelling begins a painful cycle of anger, insult and vengeance which, if repeated too often, can result in divorce.

Divorce rates give an indication of the wide scope of marital misery. Among non-Jews in the U.S. the average divorce rate is nearly 50 %.[1] Although the figure is appreciably lower among Torah observant Jews, they are not immune to this trend. According to reliable estimates, the divorce rates of Orthodox couples in the U.S. has tripled in the last twenty years, most of them divorces during the early years of marriage. This, however, does not tell the whole sad story: many more children are affected by broken marriages in this population since, in a religious household, more children are born during the early years of marriage.

Even divorce does not end the suffering of marital strife. Marriage forms a natural human unit. Because it creates so close a union between the married partners, divorce leaves wounds which do not heal easily. The lives of the divorced partners often remain shattered for a long time after they have separated, and the partners in a second marriage, which is built on the scar tissue of divorce, must work even harder to achieve success.

The lives of the children involved are even more seriously affected. Children perceive that they have been abandoned by the very people — their parents — whose role in their lives is to give them a sense of security. Their feelings of betrayal often make for a lifetime of difficulty in learning to trust other human beings.

From a Torah perspective, the divorce syndrome is very perplexing. Marriage, we are taught in the Torah, is for man's good. "לא טוב היות האדם לבדו אעשה לו עזר כנגדו" — "It is not good *(lo tov)* for man to be alone, I will make him a helpmate."[2] How could something designed by God to improve man's lot, something whose absence is described as "לא טוב" (not good) cause such misery? The Planner of the world created the perfect mechanics of the atom, the miracles of the living cell, and the precise ecological balance of nature. But with respect to the creation of man and woman something seems to have gone wrong. True, they interact perfectly on the biological level, but the planning for their emotional lives seems to have gone awry. The fact that the very institution of marriage was designed for the emotional needs of man — so that man not "be alone" — makes this even more paradoxical. For it is precisely because of emotional incompatibility that marriages are failures. What, then, happened to God's plan for overcoming man's *lo tov?*

The explanation, in short, is that marital unhappiness is caused by man's abuse of marriage. When an instrument is used without regard to the manufacturer's instructions, is it any wonder that it does not work efficiently — or that it does not work at all? Yet this is exactly what happens to marriage.

What, then, are the "manufacturer's specifications" for marriage?

Why Was Marriage Created?

Marriage is the natural state of man, as it is written, "זכר ונקבה בראם" — "[God] created them male and female."[3] Based on this verse the Sages note that an un-married individual is not a human being in the full sense of the word.[4] Since man, therefore, cannot function as a normal person outside of marriage, we can readily un-derstand why "it is not good for man to be alone."

Marriage improves every dimension of life. In fact, when we consider how many human problems marriage solves, not only does one clearly see the Divine hand behind the institution, but it appears to be nothing less than a miracle.

Man exists on a physical level, on an emotional level,

and on a spiritual level. On each of these levels, marriage provides vital benefits.

The effect of marriage on the physical level is the most obvious. Most basically, marriage solves the problem of the survival of the human species. By itself, the bearing of a new generation does not ensure human survival. To grow up normally, a human being needs a sophisticated form of nurturing in the developmental stages. For virtually his first two decades, he needs unlimited care and attention, an environment suffused with love and warmth, and constant educational guidance. None of these can be offered properly outside of marriage. The only way to develop healthy, stable individuals is to rear them within a family unit consisting of a father and a mother, who devote their unique natures and skills to the nurturing of their children. The emotional and social problems often experienced by products of broken homes are evidence of this.

The second major physical problem which marriage solves is that of the sex drive. Without marriage this potent and all-consuming drive would dominate most men's thoughts. Marriage liberates man from preoccupation with it and allows him to get on with the pursuit of his life's real goals.

But marriage is vital to man not only on the physical plane of existence, but on the emotional plane as well. By nature, man is a social being; he cannot live in solitude. Without the companionship of another human being, he suffers intensely from loneliness and is unable to function to his full capacity. Marriage not only dispels this loneliness by providing companionship but creates the possibility of the closest emotional relationship that can exist between living beings, the love between husband and wife.

Although human life would founder without the physical and emotional benefit afforded by marriage, its spiritual benefits are even more important.

Life as a Jew is inconceivable without marriage. First of all, Jewish society is based on a value system which can only survive through marriage. Generally speaking, only from within the Jewish family unit can Torah values be properly transmitted to future generations.

Just as vital as the spiritual benefits which marriage confers on the community are those which it confers upon each individual. Man was created to serve God and draw himself close to the Divine Presence. By striving towards these goals man fulfills the purposes of his creation and earns unending reward in the world-to-come. Reaching these goals is what constitutes human success in the true sense of the word.

A serious obstacle, however, stands in the way of this success: the evil inclination within man. Man's *yetzer hora* drives him to concentrate on his own physical desires, power, and prestige — in other words, to become a servant of himself rather than God. If a human being fails to stand up to these internal promptings, he will become increasingly removed from the real goals for which he was created. This *yetzer hora* is therefore a trap keeping him from the happiness and success which God intended to bestow. Consequently, the greatest gift to man is that which enables him to avoid this trap. This is precisely what marriage offers.

Marriage makes it possible for man to overcome his inclination towards self-centeredness. It permits him to change the focus of his existence from lust gratification and self-interest to that of the spiritual goal of selflessness. Marriage not only controls the sex drive, for example, it also converts it from a vehicle for the mere acquiring of pleasure to a vehicle for giving to other human beings. The sex drive becomes a means of expressing love to a wife or giving life to a child. Furthermore, marriage forces a person to cease his constant preoccupation with his own advancement and to concern himself instead with the needs of his wife and children. As he learns to become concerned with another's interests, man's drives for greed and power are slowly tempered. As a result, his personality is directed away from natural self-centeredness towards other-centeredness. This is the key to spiritual growth.

Marriage is, of course, not an immediate ticket to spiritual perfection. We see that most of mankind is afflicted by selfish obsessions despite their being married. However, marriage puts righteousness within reach. For if one chooses to use marriage properly, marriage can make a reorientation of man's aims *possible*. On the other hand, without a wife and family, man would have little hope of redeeming himself from his spiritual wasteland.

In this light, we can understand why marriage is of primary importance to Jews — perhaps even more than to any other people. True Jewish life is suffused with spiritual values which cannot flourish without marriage.

This fact lies behind the Sages' comment that "to make peace between man and wife God says, 'Let my Name written in sanctity be erased.' "[5] The Sages were referring to the commandment that a *sotah* (a suspected adulteress) drink from a special potion known as the *mey sotah* in order to clear her name and permit her to live with her husband.[6]

A *sotah* is a woman who has secluded herself with a strange man against her husband's wishes. Because of suspicious circumstances, she is forbidden to her husband until she undergoes a unique test. She drinks the *mey sotah* which causes her to die a miserable death if she has indeed committed adultery. If she does not die, this proves that she has not sinned, and she is permitted to live with her husband once again and promised a life full of blessings.

The preparation of the *mey sotah* involves erasing God's name, which, as a desecration of God's honor, is normally a grave sin. But because in this case it can reunite a wife with her husband, it is permitted. Thus, marital peace overrides the obligation to treat God's name with respect.

Now, the marital peace in question refers to a man who has a wife of questionable morality. She did, after all, seclude herself with a strange man despite her husband's objections. It is surprising that even this peace would take precedence over the honor of God's name. When we recognize, however, that man has very little potential for achieving his spiritual goals outside of marriage, we can readily understand this remarkable obligation.

God revealed his name to mankind so that man can come to a recognition of Him. What would be the point of preserving a written expression of God's name if man and wife would lose their hope of ever drawing close to the Essence which the Name represents. This is what would likely befall a couple forced to live apart by the collapse of their marriage. Alone and unable to contend with the evil inclination within themselves, they might rightly despair of ever overcoming their natural self-centeredness and the possibility of coming close to God.

Marriage, on the other hand, contains within it this hope. Consequently, preserving the potential to know God is more important than preserving the written name of God. The Creator, therefore, permits His Holy Name to be erased to enable a man and wife to continue living together. A woman once suspected of adultery is hardly an ideal wife. Yet marriage to her has more hope for spiritual achievement than no marriage at all — man living alone in a *lo tov* state.

The *Chazon Ish*[7] once told a group of students that he considered it important to have one's external appearance express one's Jewishness. The particular example he gave was growing a beard: he thought it commendable because, as he put it, "A beard is a Jewish thing."

One of the students present asked him, "Would this opinion apply to *bachurim* (unmarried young men) as well?"

"No," answered the *Chazon Ish.* "Being unmarried in itself is too un-Jewish a thing."[8]

What Is Critical for Marital Happiness?

Which of life's three levels, or components, play the most significant role in creating marital happiness — the physical, the emotional or the spiritual? Since happiness is an emotional state, we might assume that the emotional plane holds the key.

The truth is that a healthy emotional relationship in marriage depends on a proper spiritual orientation, i.e., where the couple have learned to overcome their self-ishness. This is because happiness in marriage depends on a basic element: each partner's feeling that the other is devoted to him/her. Such a relationship cannot exist between two self-centered people. It is therefore impossible for them ever to experience full marital happiness. The spiritual side of marriage, which teaches us to be concerned with another human being, is therefore what determines its emotional side. Only by learning marriage's "lesson" of increased selflessness can a couple achieve "happiness," an emotional state.

The physical relationship in marriage, of course, also plays a vital role in creating marital happiness. Besides enabling the creation of a family and the control of the sex drive, it also fosters an emotional bond between husband and wife. Marital relations awaken feelings of closeness. Indeed, the Sages have clearly indicated that the sex drive was created in man in order to provide marriage partners a means of generating love.[9]

Marital relations, however, can only arouse temporary feelings of closeness. Their capacity to generate permanent closeness depends upon the spiritual orientation (i.e., the degree of selflessness) of the marriage partners. Like a signature on a document which is valuable only in proportion to the force of the document which it endorses, marital relations have a significant effect upon the marriage bonds only in proportion to the emotions backing them up.

When the physical side of marriage is not an expression of emotion, the contrary is true: damage to the marriage results. Lust fulfillment is nothing more than selfishness; consequently, using sexual relations for the sole purpose of physical gratification will undermine the very basis of marital happiness. This sort of "love" is therefore love destined to turn to hatred — and will ultimately destroy any marriage.

Thus, on both the physical and the emotional planes, everything ultimately depends upon utilizing marriage's spiritual capacity to overcome self-centeredness.

Clearly, the "manufacturer's instructions" for marriage require that a person commit himself to developing other-centeredness, the true original goal of marriage. This is the key to marital success.

The Criteria for Choosing a Mate

Man was created to serve God by studying His word, engaging in good deeds and making the world a place in which all of mankind can come closer to Him. Therefore, the most important question in selecting a mate should be: Does this woman have the same spiritual goals as I, and will we be able to work together towards reaching these goals? Someone who does not meet these qualifications cannot possibly be considered a potential partner in life.

Jewish marriage, of course, is also aimed at building a Jewish family and ensuring the transmission of Jewish values to another generation. Serious thought should therefore be given to determining what sort of mother a prospective wife would make. Does she have the necessary qualities? What messages, overt and subtle, will she be communicating to her children? What character traits will she be displaying and encouraging her children to imitate?

Spiritual goals must be primary, but one cannot choose a wife solely on these grounds. Man is a mundane creature with mundane needs. Indeed, as we have said, marriage was especially created to satisfy these other needs as well. Without emotional and physical satisfaction in marriage, man cannot function properly.

The emotional side of marriage helps man dispel his loneliness. But it can often be more lonely living with an obnoxious person than living alone. Thus it is imperative to carefully evaluate the personality of a prospective mate: Is she pleasant to be with? Is she considerate? Is she self-centered? Does she have a temper? Does she enjoy taunting people rather than helping them?[10] The answers to these questions are vital.

How important is physical attractiveness? In light of

the above it should not be surprising that this is one of the less important considerations. For a marriage to be successful a wife does not have to be beautiful. Certainly, one cannot marry a woman whom one finds repulsive in any way (one is even forbidden to do this[11]), but physical attractiveness is by no means the critical factor for a successful marriage. If a woman possesses the proper spiritual orientation and character traits, a marriage has the capacity for producing true happiness, and a successful intimate relationship will develop as well. Physical attraction unconnected with an emotional relationship dissipates in a matter of weeks, if not days. Of primary importance in a marriage is the capacity for creating an emotional bond. Spiritual goals and personality, not physical attractiveness, are the critical factors for this.

Why, in Fact, Do Men Marry?

Despite the "manufacturer's instructions" for marriage, what qualities do most men seek in a marriage partner? Too often they are as follows:

Quality No. 1: Physical attractiveness. No matter how fit she may be for building an ideal Jewish home, no matter how sterling her character, no matter how perfect her qualifications as wife and mother, if one angle of her profile is flawed she stands a good chance of being rejected.

Quality No. 2: The impression she makes. No matter how good she may be for me, what will others think of her?

How does she measure up to my friends' wives? Will I be getting more or less than they?

Quality No. 3: Assets. What do I stand to gain from the marriage? What is there in it for me in terms of family and money?

In short, marriage is conceived of as a vehicle for appetite fulfillment and ego enhancement. In the terms of the Mishna,[12] marriage is used by man as a means for satisfying the drives for *kin'ah*, *taavah* and *kovod* (jealousy, lust and glory) — the three ways by which the *yetzer hora* expresses itself into man's life. The Sages consider these the smoothest paths to disaster: "הקנאה והתאוה והכבוד מוציאים את האדם מן העולם" — "Jealousy, lust and glory take man out of the world."[13]

Why Marriages Go Wrong

By now, it should be clear why so many marriages go wrong. God's planning has not gone awry. The marriage He created has the potential to solve man's deepest existential problems; it can provide his most profound and satisfying emotional relationship, and it can help him arrive at the pinnacle of spiritual fulfillment. But God's plan will not work unless one condition is met: that man use marriage to check his selfishness, not enhance it. If man decides to pervert marriage, the result will inevitably be the misery and disinterest in life which comes with marital unhappiness.

Marriage counselors often attempt to cure troubled marriages by advising the couple about enhancing their own physical pleasure and ego satisfaction. Nothing could be worse for a marriage. Such an approach leads them to strengthen their *yetzer hora* for selfishness instead of teaching them how to overcome it. This amounts to treating an illness by adding to its causes. Such attempts are doomed to failure. They cannot cure the ills of marriage; at most, they can create a *modus vivendi* where each partner can indulge his selfishness without interfering with the other's attempt to do the same. Such an approach is a stop-gap measure at best.

The only way to avoid — or resolve — marital discord is by building the marriage in accordance with its original plan, by using marriage as a vehicle for becoming concerned with another human being's welfare. The only counselling which can be effective is that which teaches marriage partners to become selflessly concerned with *each other's* pleasure and ego feelings — even at the expense of their own. Marriage will then become all God intended it to be: an instrument of human perfection and happiness.

NOTES TO CHAPTER TWO

1. Statistical Abstract of the U.S., 1984.
2. *Bereyshis 2:18.*
3. *Ib. 1:27.*
4. *Yevamos 63a.*
5. *Sukkah 53b.*
6. *Bamidbar Chap. 5.*
7. Leading Torah sage of his time; d. 5714/1954.
8. Based on interview.
9. *Shabbos 152b;* cf. R. Moshe Cordovero, *Tomer Devorah,* Chapter 6.
10. *Yevamos 63a; Rashi ib. s.v. meson.*
11. *Kiddushin 51a.*
12. *Avos 4, 21.*
13. *Ib.*

3

FANTASY AND REALITY IN MARRIED LIFE

Some of the major problems of marriage are rooted in the unrealistic expectations with which marriage is entered into. Therefore, before setting out to describe in detail what marriage should be, we must first spell out what marriage is *not*.

Marriage is not the fantasy world which newly married couples believe it is. While fantasies are not real, they are not necessarily harmless. If the fantasies are not put to rest quickly, the shock of disillusionment can be disastrous.

The Fantasies and Their Causes

The major fantasy about marriage is that it confers eternal bliss. Two corollaries follow from this: (1) that married people are constantly in love, and (2) that spouses have no faults.

Fantasies, like all dreams, are largely forms of vicarious wish-fulfillment. Thus, whatever our innermost desires — lust, power, prestige, or even the spiritual goals of Torah acquisition and character perfection — we fantasize that marriage will achieve them all for us.

The fantasy of marriage as eternal bliss thrives especially among those who have grown up under the influence of Western values. From their early years, children are informed that the close company of a woman produces quick and permanent ecstasy. (It is no coincidence that in the popular songs heard in America, the word "love" often rhymes with "above" in the phrase "heaven above.") The victim of too many of these messages naturally expects to find instant bliss in marriage.

Another cause of fantasies about marriage is the sex drive itself, viewed by many single young men as their most troublesome problem. Because it overshadows all else, they are led to believe that when they find relief from it through marriage their lives will be problem free. This is, of course, naive. Coping with the sex drive is only one of life's many challenges — as the difficulties of married people so plainly testify. A single person, however, does not easily see things this way; he perceives this as his only problem. Hence the fantasy of everlasting bliss.

Unfortunately, misinterpretations of selective readings from the Torah and the Talmud do their part as well in bolstering marriage fantasies. Man, we are taught, is a half-person without a wife.[1] The Torah teaches us that a woman is man's lost "rib";[2] therefore, it is thought that man and wife are meant to fit together as perfectly as a rib in a body. Furthermore, since woman is man's *aveydah* (lost object),[3] marriage will confer all the joy of having a lost part of oneself restored.

In addition, the Sages say that "whoever lives without a wife lives without joy, without blessing, and without Torah learning."[4] This seems to imply that with a wife, the way is automatically clear for the converse: unbounded joy, limitless blessing, and greatness in Torah.

The Sages also say that "forty days before the conception of the fetus a heavenly voice calls out, 'So-and-so will marry so-and-so.'"[5] A wife is therefore preordained by Divine decree, and is obviously intended to meet man's every need. She certainly can have no characteristic which will cause her husband displeasure. For do not the Sages say, "אשה כשרה עושה רצון בעלה" — "A righteous woman does the will of her husband"?[6] And does not the Rambam write that a wife should treat her husband as a lord?[6a] Thus the fantasy emerges that a wife will automatically cater to every whim and desire of her husband and that she will be able to intuit his every wish even before he voices it. When not serving him, she will find no greater joy than gazing at him with adoration.

To the many young men beguiled by these fantasies, it is practically axiomatic that life's goals will be realized early in married life. This applies especially to spiritual goals. Through the husband's conversations with his wife on their dates and through discussion with others, he has ascertained beyond any doubt that her greatest desire is to live according to the ideals of Judaism. He is buoyantly confident that their future home will be a bastion of learning, kindness, sanctity, and mutual devotion.

The speeches at the wedding and the week-long *Sheva Berachos* celebrations add the finishing threads to his tapestry of expectations. The bride is compared to the greatest women in Jewish history; her character is "flawless"; her good heart is "unequalled." He will become a latter-day Rabbi Akiva who achieved greatness in Torah by virtue of his wife's devotion to his learning.[7]

The Disillusionment Process

Unfortunately, the fantasies are short-lived. Slowly, but inevitably, the shocking truth sets in.

The physical attraction begins to lose its initial excitement. The wife who no longer preens herself and wears a different dress for each meeting, appears somehow less attractive.

Her attitude towards him has changed for the worse. Probably as a result of being able to see him daily from close up, her admiration has grown thinner. She no longer accepts his opinions uncritically and often even claims to know better than he.

She is not at all the perfect human being he thought he was marrying. There are obvious flaws. She is not as calm and relaxed as he knew her to be on their dates. She can be shrill and panicky; she can be stubborn and illogical.

Especially disturbing is the absence of that surge of accomplishment and wisdom which he had expected to materialize once the fetters of bachelorhood were cast off.

Worst of all, he sometimes feels lonely. He cannot share so much of life with her. She does not appreciate his words of Torah. She does not accept his opinions. She does not grasp his jokes. She does not like the same music. She has different tastes in clothing and in home furnishings.

He often wishes he were single again and in the company of his old friends. He had it much better then. There were no bills to be paid, far fewer distractions, no wife who needed constant attention, no decisions weighing on his mind.

As the fantasies dissipate, terrifying questions begin to insinuate themselves into his mind. Is she the right one? If overcoming loneliness is what marriage is all about, why is he so lonely? Can she be the preordained wife of forty days before conception if he still has problems?

The questions gnaw at him. Because he is too ashamed to share them with anyone, they fester within him. Disappointment and hurt begin to seep through his entire emotional fabric. He suspects that his marriage was a mistake; he feels trapped by it and wonders if it will last.

He begins to feel resentment towards his wife for having concealed her true nature from him before they were married. The resentment breeds an anger which grows within him.

One day, he feels he can no longer tolerate her inability to make him happy, and his disillusionment and bitterness, triggered by some trivial matter, pour out in a spasm of rage.

The wife is shocked and grievously hurt. The man she loves, and who she thought loved her, has now turned on her without good reason. Before long, her shock gives rise to bitterness and anger and she retaliates. A cycle of attack and counterattack is set into motion, with its tragic potential.

What Is the Reality?

The only problem which marriage solves is the problem of bachelorhood. Granted, this is not an unimportant problem because man is too lonely, too rootless, and too distracted to be able to address himself to the real challenges of life without marriage. But marriage itself provides no ultimate answers; it is simply the best framework for dealing with the problems of living.

If life presents difficulties, this should not be surprising. Life is meant to be a series of challenges. There is no lasting bliss on this earth. What matters is that we meet these challenges properly, for then we will have accomplished our purpose in creation. As the Sages say, "היום לעשותם ומחר לקבל שכרם" — "Today [this world] is for work; tomorrow [the world-to-come] is for the bliss of reward."[7a] One has to operate within the natural state of existence called marriage to meet the challenges of life.

The Reality of Love

Rabbi Leib Chasman, famous *baal mussar* and *mashgiach* (spiritual supervisor) of Chevron Yeshivah, once saw a student eating fish with great relish. "Tell me, young man," he asked him, "do you love fish?" The *bochur* answered in the affirmative. "If you love fish," replied Reb Leib, "then you should have cared for the one on your plate; you should have fed it and tried to make it happy. Instead you are devouring it." As the student groped for a proper response, Reb Leib explained: "Obviously, you don't love fish. You love yourself!"[8]

Reb Leib was trying to drive home the point that what most people call "love" is really self-love. The love sold on the billboards and television screens of the world is merely the selfish love of pleasure fulfillment. The romance portrayed as an ideal is so often just a glorification of some of man's baser instincts, a fantasy of physical and emotional gratification.

Real love, in contrast, exists where one is willing to give up something dear to him for the benefit of another person. Developing a relationship of love is not an instant process. One cannot love unless something has triggered that love. When a person feels gratitude for benefits which another person has rendered him, when he finds noble qualities in another, when he senses that someone is devoted to him unconditionally — only then can he truly and completely love that person.[9]

Not surprisingly, this form of love does not come about during the early stages of marriage. Two strangers who have met each other a limited number of times before becoming husband and wife cannot possibly enjoy this degree of mutual devotion. Love in its true sense is only possible between two people who have spent many years sharing experiences, working towards common goals, undergoing sacrifices for each other, and building a life together. It must be realized that this can take decades.

This is why the early years of marriage are the most difficult, and why most divorces occur during this period. For this reason (among others), the Torah commands a man to spend the first year of marriage making his wife happy. [10] As the author of the *Sefer HaChinuch* explains, a man and wife, who start out as nearly total strangers, need time to get used to one other. [11] A newly married couple needs more work during the first year of marriage than at any other stage of their married life in learning to be mutually compatible. This obligation reflects the reality of marriage and shows the naivete of expecting love to begin simultaneously with the breaking of the wedding glass.

Marriage cannot begin with true love. What should be present at the outset, however, is a strong commitment by both partners to devote themselves to helping each other and serving as each other's lifelong friend. This means that a husband must undertake to treat his wife as well as he would treat himself: to fulfill her physical and emotional needs; to ensure her happiness; to deny her nothing he would not deny himself; and to treat her with due respect. All of this is contained in the Sages' prescription of the duties of a husband to his wife: "He must love her as himself and honor her more than himself." [12] This means that he has to satisfy her needs as much as he satisfies his own, and he must concern himself with making her feel as respectable in his — as well as the public's — eyes, even more than he concerns himself with his own needs and respectability.

Because this commitment will make each partner feel

that his/her spouse genuinely cares about him/her, it is the first step and the surest way of building the emotional bond which will lead to a happy marriage.

This is possibly why the prophet Malachi calls a wife "חברתך ואשת בריתך" — "Your comrade and wife of your covenant."[13] The term "comrade" alludes to the first step of marriage, the commitment to devotion and friendship made at its outset. "Covenant," on the other hand, alludes to the sense of unity felt by the parties to a covenant. Marriage as covenant is marriage imbued with the love which creates this sensation of unity. The order in this verse, first "comrade" and then "wife of your covenant" is significant and refers to the way a marriage develops. If the first stage, "for she is your comrade" — with its implicit commitment to keep the marriage obligations — is kept, the marriage will then develop into the next stage where she will become the "wife of your covenant."

Note that "falling in love" is not a pre-condition for getting married; needed is an honest commitment to be totally devoted to a wife's needs. Even if strong emotions are lacking at the beginning of a marriage, this commitment will foster love. "כמים הפנים לפנים" — "A person's attitude is the reflected image of his friend's attitude towards him."[14] Acting with commitment towards a wife will set into motion a process which will inevitably lead to a deep emotional attachment.

Admittedly, the commitment of devotion is not an easy one to make and to keep. Man has an innate selfishness which drives him to exploit everything and everyone around him for his own gratification. His natural inclination will therefore be to satisfy his own needs at his wife's expense, not to give up too much for her needs. But every time he acts selfishly, the foundations of a successful marital relationship are undermined. For only through working to overcome this tendency can a marriage ever prosper.

The Reality of Faults in a Wife

One of the early tests of a husband's commitment to his wife occurs when he discovers her faults. Whether the fault is as petty as her forgetting to replace the cover of the toothpaste tube or as irritating as an emotional weakness, or a lack of: intelligence, decision making ability, household skills, beauty without makeup, etc., the discovery can make a husband panic. He is suddenly disabused of the fantasies with which he entered marriage. He had expected to pride himself on having a perfect wife, both the most attractive and the one who would make an excellent impression on his friends. In short, he thought that his wife would supply him with full satisfaction of his basic *kin'ah*, *taavah* and *kovod* (jealousy, pleasure and glory) drives. He now tells himself that he made a mistake in marrying her.

He fails to understand, however, that his disillusionment stems from a faulty conception of marriage. As noted earlier, marriage is God's precious gift to man. It was created to teach him to become selfless and to enable him to vanquish loneliness. In contrast, *kin'ah*, *taavah* and *kovod* are man's greatest enemies. Rather than reacting to the discovery of a fault with the feeling, "What a miscreant I've married," one should remind himself that marriage is his only hope to live as a normal human being. If a husband would make a list of all the faults he has discovered in his wife and weigh them against the fact that his wife has committed herself to loving him and serving as his closest companion for a lifetime — despite all *his* faults, all complaints would vanish in their insignificance. Because marriage is so vital, the discovery of a fault in a wife simply means that one has discovered something with which he has to learn to live. It has to be looked upon as another challenge of marriage — and of life itself.

This is what the Sages meant when they said: "אתתך גוצא גחין ולחיש לה" — "If your wife is short, bend down and whisper to her."[15] This means, if your wife does not understand you, do not become annoyed with her; instead, make an extra effort to explain yourself. Your commitment to treat her with respect does not change because she has a fault.

It is interesting to note that not only do the Sages enjoin us to ignore faults in a wife, they even consider slight faults to be an asset in marriage. "נחות דרגא ונסוב איתתא" — "Descend a step and marry a woman,"[16] they say. Because a husband is relentlessly driven by his male ego, he will often be tempted to prove his superiority, a tendency which might easily trigger domestic strife. A wife with a fault lessens this temptation. Being married to a woman perceived to be less "perfect" than oneself is thus, ironically, not undesirable. Though his perception may be erroneous, at the very least it feeds his ego needs.

The only way to avoid disillusionment would be to

enter marriage realistically. Weaknesses and faults are endemic to human beings, and choosing a marriage partner really means deciding which faults one decides to live with.

The Concept of the "Basherte" ("The Intended")

When the Sages tell us that everyone has a wife preordained for him forty days before conception (popularly known as one's *"basherte"*), they do not mean that this woman is faultless. They mean, rather, that by marrying one another, these two people would best be able to carry out their purposes in life.

Every person must strive to reach certain goals in his lifetime: goals for which he as an individual was created, and goals which he has as a member of the Jewish people. Not everyone is meant to play the same role in life. Some people are created to live in wealth, others in poverty; some are meant to be healthy, others weak and beset with illness; everyone is given a set of challenges which he must meet.

One's intended *basherte* is the woman through whom one will be able to carry out his ultimate goals, whatever they are. Again, this does not imply that a wife must be perfect. Indeed, it may well be that her husband's purpose in life is to overcome the annoyance caused him by her shortcoming. In other words, her faults may be an opportunity and a challenge for her husband to learn tolerance and patience.

One of the examples which the Talmud gives for the *basherte* concept is Delilah, wife of Shimshon.[17] Certainly, Delilah was very far from being an ideal wife. Not only did she neglect her husband's happiness, she even tried to undermine his life's goal of redeeming his people from oppression — and eventually contributed to his death. Nevertheless, she was still his *basherte* because she was the woman through whom Shimshon was meant to carry out his purpose in life. And, in fact, the temptations of Delilah were what ultimately permitted Shimshon to serve God to the utmost.[18]

Ultimately, the concept of *basherte* has little practical bearing on everyday life.[19] Proving that a woman is or is not one's *basherte* is simply not possible. It certainly makes no sense to conclude from a woman's behavior that marrying her was a mistake.

If a man is fortunate enough to marry his *basherte*,[20] this does not free him from his obligations as a Jew, in particular from the necessity of controlling his selfish instincts and his anger. Furthermore even marriage to a *basherte* can end in divorce if one fails to uphold his marital obligations or to act decently toward his pre-ordained wife.

"A Righteous Woman"

When the Sages and Rambam say that a righteous woman does the will of her husband or that she treats him like a lord,[21] they are not implying that in an ideal household a husband has no obligations or restrictions, and that he may act to his heart's desires. A Jew's life is replete with obligations and restrictions, particularly his married life. The very next sentence of the Rambam makes this clear:

"A husband must love his wife as himself and honor her more than himself."

When they said that a righteous woman does the will of her husband, the Sages meant to offer a wife advice on how to contribute to peace in her household. Since the male ego drives a man to assert his superiority — which constitutes a constant threat to peace in the home, a wife would do well to nullify this threat by acknowledging her husband's superiority. This does not necessarily mean that this is a wife's obligation or that this must be her natural reaction. It also does not mean she should acquiesce to acts by her husband which are not compatible with the Torah. But it does mean that it is an excellent way for her to defuse the source of much potential anger. This advice, of course, does not free the husband from his obligations. He is required to be doing his utmost to keep from succumbing to his craving for superiority. Obviously, when both husband and wife act in this manner, there will be very few areas of disagreement remaining.

The true implication of the other above-cited statement of the Sages should be noted as well. "Whoever lives without a wife lives without joy, without blessing, without Torah learning,"[22] does not mean that as soon as a person marries, all of these gifts descend upon him miraculously. Hard work towards spiritual growth, and hard work alone, confers joy, blessing, and Torah. The Sages are merely stating that without marriage one could not even begin to work towards this growth. Achieving it, however, is not automatic; it requires much struggle and self-control.

NOTES TO CHAPTER THREE

1. *Yevamos 63a.*
2. *Bereyshis 2:21.*
3. *Kiddushin 2b.*
4. *Yevamos 62b.*
5. *Sota 2a.*
6. *Tanna Devei Eliyahu Rabba 9; Rambam Ishus 15:20.*
7. *Kesubos 62b.*
7a. *Eyruvin 22a.*
8. From an eyewitness.
9. Vilna Gaon, *Commentary to Shir HaShirim 5:2;* this is discussed more at length in Chapter Eleven.
10. *Devorim 24:5.*
11. *Chinuch No. 581.*
12. *Yevamos 62b; Rambam Ishus 15:19.*
13. *Malachi 2:14.*
14. *Mishley 27:19.*
15. *Bava Metzia 59a.*
16. *Yevamos 63a.*
17. *Shoftim Chapter 14 ff.*
18. *Ib. 16.*
19. See *Rambam, Shemonah Perakim, Chap. 8.*
20. See *Mo'ed Katan 18b* that one may not merit marrying her.
21. *Tanna Devei Eliyahu Rabba 9; Rambam Ishus 15:20.*
22. *Yevamos 62b.*

4

LEARNING THE BASICS

The first step in marriage is creating the elemental relationship which should exist between any two people who are living together. It is, unfortunately, necessary to emphasize that a wife deserves to be treated no less decently than, say, a roommate, coworker or travelling companion. One must take pains to ensure that consideration, politeness, courtesy, appreciation — and all that goes by the name of civilized conduct — are not compromised once the fiancée becomes the wife.

I know of a great Yeshivah teacher who would call in each of his students before they were married to tell them not to forget to say "please" to their wives upon requesting something from them and "have a pleasant day" upon leaving the house. This teacher should be hailed for his wisdom in recognizing the need for this basic advice, for the neglect of such common-sense behavior is quite widespread.

Some might argue that this sort of formality can create an artificial atmosphere which inhibits the intimacy which should prevail in a home. It is true that formality has no place in marriage,[1] but politeness need not be a culprit. Saying "excuse me," "thank you," and "good morning" is an accepted norm of human behavior — and for a good reason. These express one person's respect for, and concern with, the feelings of another. Because this way of acting makes a wife feel she is not taken for granted, it builds intimacy in a very real way.

Besides politeness, other forms of behavior which we employ in ordinary social contexts also have their place in a marriage. We are, for example, required to be as pleasant in a wife's company as we are in the company of strangers. The Rambam writes that a husband should never be sad in his wife's presence.[2] Among strangers we try to demonstrate our good humor and portray ourselves as permanently cheerful; we are no less obliged to do so at home. Acting in this manner creates the warm and friendly atmosphere necessary to nurture a successful marriage. One of the greatest Torah sages of our times, speaking from a spiritual standpoint, advised a newly married young man to emphasize a light and relaxed attitude which, he said, is often more valuable to a marriage than seriousness.[3]

A husband is obligated to treat his wife with at least as much respect as he gives to others. The most basic way to show respect to a wife is to pay attention to her when she speaks; this is a demonstration of respect for her. To listen with half an ear is a good way to insult her — or anyone else, for that matter.

A young man who came to Judaism in his adult years

— now a teacher of Torah himself — told me that his deepest impression of Jewish life, one which brought him closest to Torah was made while he was the Shabbos guest of a certain learned rabbi. He noticed that this rabbi (who happens to be a world-famous personality) never failed to react to, or comment respectfully upon, anything his wife would say. The rabbi was obviously in the habit of demonstrating his regard for her. More than anything else this sensitivity, which was so clearly a product of the rabbi's learning and outlook on life, attracted this young man to the ways of the Torah.

The Interpersonal Mitzvos

More important is another obvious, yet ignored, truth: all the commandments which a Jew is enjoined to observe in his relations with his fellow man (the *beyn odom lachaveyro* mitzvos) apply no less to one's wife. As a matter of fact, should a conflict arise in carrying out these mitzvos for the benefit of either a wife or a stranger, a wife would take precedence. One is obligated to do charity or *chessed* for one's relatives before strangers.[4]

It is therefore appropriate to record here some of the interpersonal mitzvos which frequently come into play in marriage.

1) "ואהבת לרעך כמוך" — "Love your fellow as yourself."[5] This refers, of course, to a wife as well as to anyone else. This commandment obligates a Jew to help the weak, comfort the sad, and try to make peace between quarrelling parties — even if the weak, the sad, or the party to a quarrel happens to be one's wife. Anyone who

treats another person, including his wife, in a manner in which he himself would not enjoy being treated violates this commandment.[6]

According to Rabbeynu Yonah, this mitzvah also requires a person to spend time thinking about how to improve his fellow's lot.[7]

So central is this mitzvah to Jewish life, that Hillel considered it the key to the entire Torah. The rest of the Torah, he said, is merely an elaboration upon it.[8]

In addition to the general obligation to love a fellow Jew, there is an additional obligation to love a wife as oneself, and to honor her more than oneself.[9]

2) "ושמח את אשתו" — "One should make his wife happy."[10] This is a special requirement, in addition to those listed below, to pay physical and emotional attention to a wife during the first year of marriage.[11] (For example, according to the author of the *Sefer HaChinuch* one should not leave home for an extended period during this first year.[12]) One opinion holds that this special commandment applies throughout marriage.[13]

3) "בצדק תשפוט עמיתך" — "Judge your fellow fairly."[14] This commandment obligates us to give others the benefit of the doubt.[15] If the fellow in question is God-fearing we must assume that he acted with worthy intent even if it would be more plausible to assume the opposite. The commandment naturally applies to a wife: whatever she does — or fails to do — has to be interpreted as well-intended.

4) "והלכת בדרכיו" — "You shall follow in His ways."[16] We are obligated to develop in ourselves kindness and compassion, God's way of relating to mankind.[17] Thus we must be kind and compassionate to our wives, abstaining from anger.

In addition to these positive commandments. The following prohibitions are also commonly applicable:

5) "עונתה לא יגרע" — "You shall not diminish her appointed time."[18] It is forbidden to refrain from keeping one's obligations to engage in marital relations in a manner and time which satisfies a wife's emotional needs.[19]

6) "לא תשנא את אחיך בלבבך" — "You shall not hate your brother in your heart."[20] One violates this prohibition by harboring feelings of hatred towards any person. According to the Rambam one does not violate this prohibition if he verbalizes his negative feelings, since they are not then "in our hearts."[21]

7) "לא תונו איש את עמיתו" — "You may not verbally oppress your fellow."[22] This forbids one from making any statement to a fellow Jew which causes him emotional pain.[23] If, for example, someone's relative has been hanged, one is forbidden to ask him to hang something (such as a fish) on a rope, lest he become embarrassed by suspecting that others listening are reminded of his relative's fate.[24] It goes without saying that every time someone gets into an argument with his wife and hurts her feelings he is violating this prohibition.

8) "לא תשא שמע שוא" — "You shall not bear slanderous

tales."[25] This is the prohibition against *loshon hora* which includes saying anything derogatory about another Jew, whether to his face or behind his back.[26]

9-10) "לא תקום ולא תטור" — "You shall not take revenge; you shall not remember the evil which your friend has done to you [even without taking revenge]."[27] One is forbidden to say to a wife, "I will not act the way you have acted to me in the past."[28] Certainly, it is forbidden to actually retaliate for physical or verbal injuries she has inflicted on him in the past.[29]

11) "לא תקלל חרש" — "You shall not curse a deaf person."[30] This is the prohibition against cursing another Jew.[31]

Finally, there is the prohibition from the *kesuvim* (Hagiographa):

12) "לא יהיה בך אל זר" — "You shall not have a false god within you."[32] The Sages say this refers to the *yetzer hora* (the evil inclination) within a person, in particular to the evil inclination which causes one to become angry, which is considered as if it were a form of idolatry.[33]

Why Wives Are Treated Worse Than Strangers

Of course, the *beyn odom lachaveyro* mitzvos are the most difficult ones to observe, and therefore even religiously observant Jews are often derelict in this area. Because awareness of these mitzvos is easily buried under selfish concerns, we need to be continuously reminded and encouraged to observe them. This is especially relevant with respect to applying them *vis-a-vis* one's wife.

Many people are aware of the importance of *chessed* (kindness). They make it a point to help others, to have guests for Shabbos, and to advise and support as many people as they can. These same people, however, often forget that there is an equal mitzvah of *chessed* to satisfy a wife's legitimate needs. For example:

A husband wants to have a *sheva berachos* party in his home for his newly married friend. His wife, overburdened with the double responsibility of caring for her children and holding down a job, cannot undertake this extra burden — and she objects to making the party. The husband may become resentful and may even insist angrily that it be held.

While a very great mitzvah of *chessed* is at stake here — making a bride and groom happy — protecting a wife from working beyond her strength is no less a mitzvah of *chessed*. Furthermore, engaging in a quarrel over this matter could involve many serious transgressions.[34] Yet it seems obvious to too many husbands that kindness to others takes precedence.

The underlying reason for this wrongheaded attitude is that one acquires a certain amount of prestige or regard by helping persons outside the family unit. Few people are as ready to get out of bed at 3 A.M. to rock a baby (who deserves *chessed* no less than any other being) as to assist an old lady across the street at 3 P.M. Similarly, few husbands consider making a pleasant remark to raise a harried wife's spirits as important as engaging in pleasantry with a total stranger. Doing *chessed* privately, where there are no fringe benefits of social recognition, is much more difficult.

This does not mean, of course, that one should do kindness only when no trace of self-interest is involved. On the contrary, the Sages teach us that one should perform mitzvos even for the wrong reason *(shelo lishma)* because one will ultimately acquire purity of motive *(lishma).*[35] But it does explain why certain mitzvos generally performed in private, like being kind to a wife, are often slighted.

Not only is neglect of *chessed* to a wife wrong in itself, it can even invalidate the mitzvah to which the husband gives precedence. Although the Sages instructed us to engage in mitzvos no matter what our intentions are, this holds true only as long as the performance of the mitzvah does not violate another mitzvah. For if one does commit a transgression together with a mitzvah, another principle comes into play: that a mitzvah done simultaneously with a transgression is not valid, under the principle of *mitzvah ha-ba'ah ba'aveyrah.*[36] Kindness at another person's expense, especially a wife's, is often a classic example of this principle.

The Barometer of True Kindness

The best barometer of one's goodheartedness is usually the *chessed* which one does in private. An individual who is kinder to strangers than to his family has a spiritual problem which calls for serious self-examination.

Rav Elchonon Wasserman in his eulogy of his master, the Chafetz Chayim, made the following point:

Most famous gentiles, he said, are the subject of many impressive stories. It is well-known, however, that when one begins investigating their private lives, the stories are often quite sordid. Not infrequently, the generals, presidents or artists portrayed as great human beings during their lifetimes emerge as brutes when the true story of their lives is told. (Beethoven is a case in point.) But with respect to Jewish *tzaddikim*, the contrary is true. One has no idea of their true greatness until the story of their private lives is told.

The reason for this phenomenon, explained Reb Elchonon, is that the great and the famous are, more often than not, driven to do good things by the desire for fame and recognition. They are happy to act selflessly as long as people are watching; in private, however, they revert to their natural selfishness. On the other hand, a *tzaddik* does good not to make an impression on others, but because this is the will of God. He therefore tries to hide his good deeds from the public eye so as not to detract from their purity. As a result, the more we enter a *tzaddik's* personal life the more we recognize his true saintliness.

The Chafetz Chayim's life is a case in point. His many important works dealing with the interpersonal mitzvos brought him fame. And many legends abounded about his meticulous care in keeping these mitzvos. But all these dwarfed the true story of the kindliness which he showed in his private life.

The degree in which one's private behavior differs from his public behavior is an excellent way to measure one's true spiritual level.

NOTES TO CHAPTER FOUR

1 Letter by Chazon Ish ז״ל (Rabbi A. Y. Karelitz, d. Cheshvan 5714/1954, foremost halachic authority of his generation); published many times, most recently in *"Veyadata ki shalom ohalecha,"* p. 12, by the late Rabbi Chayim Friedlander, Bnei Brak, 5746.

2. *Rambam, Ishus 15:19.*

3. Letter cited in Note 1.

4. *Rambam, Matnos Aniyim, 7:13; Shulchan Aruch Yoreh Deah, 241:3.*

5. *Vayikra 19:18.*

6. *Shabbos 31a.*

7. Rabbeynu Yonah, *Shaarey Teshuvah* Sec. III, par. 138.

8. *Shabbos ib.*

9. *Yevamos 62b; Rambam, Ishus ib.*

10. *Devarim 24:5.*

11. *Sota 43a.*

12. *Sefer HaChinuch 582.*

13. *SeMaK 285* based on *Pesachim 72b;* see *Nishmas Odom* to *Chayyei Odom 147, 1.*

14. *Vayikra 19:15.*

15. *Sefer HaChinuch 235.*

16. *Devorim 28:9.*

17. *Rambam, Deyos 1:6-7; Chinuch 611.*

18. *Shemos 21:10.*

19. See *Commentary of Ramban* to *Shemos ib.*

20. *Vayikra 19:17.*

21. *Rambam Deyos 6:5; Chinuch 238.*

22. *Vayikra 25:17.*

23. *Bava Metzia 58b: Rambam, Mechira 14:12; Chinuch 338.*

24. *Bava Metzia 59b.*

25. *Vayikra 19:16.*

26. *Rambam Deyos 7:1; Chinuch 236.*

27. *Vayikra 19:18.*

28. *Yoma 23a; Rambam, Deyos 7:8; Chinuch 242.*

29. *Yoma ib; Rambam ib. 7:7; Chinuch 241.*

30. *Vayikra 19:14.*

31. *Rambam, Sanhedrin 26:1; Chinuch 231.*

32. *Tehillim 81.*

33. *Shabbos 105b.*   34. See above.   35. *Nazir 23b.*

36. *Sukkah 30a.*

5

RECOGNIZING THE FEMALE NATURE

For man to live in peace with his wife he must recognize and appreciate her female nature. Men and women were given different roles in life and, in particular, in the creation of the family unit. Not only were they given different bodies for these roles, they were given different emotional and intellectual systems as well. These result in different approaches in many areas, approaches which often cause domestic friction. If men would understand women better and respond accordingly, much of this friction could be eliminated.

The Need to Be Admired

A woman's most deep-seated need, the one which shapes her personality and attitude toward life more than anything else, is her need to be loved, admired, and respected.[1] To be sure, getting attention and making a good impression are also quite important to men, but to women they are absolutely vital. Unwanted and uncared for, a woman feels she is something less than a human being.

Two of the great sages of our times, writing on the guidelines for marital happiness, emphasize the fact that "a woman's nature is to find favor in her husband's eyes,"[2] and that "giving a woman the feeling that she is unloved is akin to spilling her blood."[3]

This is why the Sages say that a woman desires to be married more than a man does and — as a result — is not as particular as a man in choosing a mate. A woman's attitude in choosing a mate, the Sages say, is "טב למיתב טן דו מלמיתב ארמלו" — "It is better to live as a twosome than to live like a widow."[4] A marital relationship is important for a man, but to a woman it is essential: marriage more than anything else satisfies her core need to be admired and loved. Outside of marriage she feels "like a widow." It is no wonder that, as can be commonly seen, women suffer more deeply following a divorce than men: loneliness apparently affects them more than men.

Beginning relatively early in childhood, females are more concerned about their appearance than males. Little girls, for example, care more about their clothing — even their handwriting — than do little boys. That girls are toilet-trained earlier than boys[5] may well be related to this same female characteristic.

Of course, female concern with appearance only intensifies as the girl matures, and one of her highest priorities throughout life is her attractiveness.

The size of the women's fashion industry, an industry devoted to a large extent to making women attractive to men, attests to this. The styles, cuts, colors — and the rate at which women's fashions change — leave little doubt that most women choose clothing to make themselves pleasing and eye-catching.

While men are also interested in their clothing, their perspective is decidedly different. Through their clothing women tend to communicate the message, "Please look at me." Men's clothing, in contrast, is meant to gain respect, prestige or to display a certain image — dignified, young, rich, et al. Rarely is the intent to attract attention. This is what Rabbi Yochanan meant when he said that clothing are man's "honorers."[6] They are the means by which others identify one's status in the community, causing him honor. Women's clothing would, accordingly, be called, their "attractors."

Torah law does not make light of women's special interest in clothes. A husband is obligated to make his wife happy on a festival by buying her "בגדים צבעונים" — colored clothing.[7] Simple, white garments are not enough to make a woman's heart glad; it is necessary to supply her with "colored" clothing, i.e., clothing which makes her attractive to her husband.

Showing Affection and Appreciation

A husband should go to great lengths to make sure that his wife feels loved and cared for. Nothing shocks a new wife more than the suspicion that her husband may not love her as much as she had hoped. This is not surprising since, as the quotation cited above has put it, the pain of this realization is "akin to spilling her blood."

Quite obviously, this should never happen in the home of a Jewish man committed to doing *chessed* to every Jew, especially the wife whose happiness he has specifically undertaken to enhance in marriage. It is unconscionable to give her the slightest grounds for this suspicion.

A wise husband can therefore never afford to stop demonstrating that he cares for his wife. And he is not likely to if he makes a conscious effort to pay serious attention to the various favors and benefits he receives from her. We have previously noted that common courtesy calls for expressing gratitude for favors received. But showing simple gratitude is not enough; it is necessary to shower her with praise for this. Because a wife needs to feel that she is beloved, her husband should leave her no room for doubt. Compliments and praise are the elemental way of creating this consciousness.

One of my teachers carried this principle to what some might call "extremes." Shortly after his marriage, his wife served him burnt potatoes for supper. Instead of complaining, he told her, "Oh, what a wonderful dish you've made tonight." His wife was so pleased that she made him the same "dish" many suppers afterwards, each of which he duly complimented, although it was becoming more and more difficult for him to eat the burnt potatoes. When my teacher saw that there was no other way out of the dilemma he had created for himself, he finally told her, "You know, my dear wife, let's try something new. One can get tired of anything."

Of course, any compliment which sounds contrived will make any woman (or man) feel she is being patronized rather than loved, but in the final analysis most people will agree that even an invented compliment is better than none at all.

In point of fact, however, there is no need to invent them. By merely becoming aware of all the good bestowed by one's wife, one will find no shortage of reasons for which to praise her.

Nor need a compliment be merely verbal. A smile, a note, or a small gift can eloquently express one's feelings of appreciation and love. I know of someone who could barely afford to buy bread for his table, but whenever he would pass a pretty flower growing in an empty lot, he would bring it home to his wife. Despite financial hardships, his wife was a happy woman.

One should never assume that his appreciation is so obvious that it need not be expressed. It is painfully difficult for a wife to divine her husband's unexpressed feelings.

Criticism

One of the most painful things a husband can do is to criticize his wife in the wrong manner. Although no one enjoys being criticized, a woman suffers much more than a man does from criticism given with anger. Criticizing a wife in the wrong way is the equivalent of telling her that she is unattractive or is unloved. Because of her need to be admired, a woman is tortured by such criticism.

Unfortunately, many husbands think it their solemn duty to correct every single fault. This is a potentially disastrous mistake. The fact is that the criticism often derives from the husband's own need to feel strong and powerful — and obeyed.

In speaking with a husband with serious domestic difficulties, I asked what he usually discussed with his wife. He proudly told me that conversation was one of the strong points of his marriage. Whenever they sat down to dinner together, they never wasted time on idle chatter. He usually made sure to talk about the things he thought she had done wrong during the day.

It was immediately obvious what was wrong with their marriage. I advised the husband to change his approach and talk instead about the positive things his wife had done during the day. I also advised him to spend more time in friendly chatter to make his wife happier and more relaxed. Happily, their relationship was enhanced considerably.

Nothing triggers domestic quarrelling more than harsh criticism. As with anything too painful to bear, criticism evokes defensive reactions — and a predictable pattern of response follows. The wife will either deny the fault her husband has attributed to her or will counter with an accusation that he has worse faults. When he hears her denying the truth of his criticism, he begins to argue his point more vehemently. As she sees him growing angry over what she considers a trivial matter, she is convinced of what she suspected all along: he really does not love her. On the other hand, her denials prompt the husband to think that she is really dishonest. As a woman who would rather argue than become better, she is, he concludes, undeserving of any respect. This kind of imbroglio could lead to marital disaster.

As we have previously indicated, a husband should not feel obligated to correct every fault he discovers in his wife. On the contrary, he must learn to live with them. If criticism is warranted, it has to be constructive and presented with endearment, without any implication that the wife is less beloved because of the particular fault.

For example, if a wife frequently leaves a bag of groceries in a place where her husband trips over it, the worst reaction is: "Can't you ever think about what you're doing? Why do you *always* have to make me trip?"

A much wiser and more effective response would be: "I realize you don't have enough space or time to put everything away in this apartment. Maybe we can build more shelves or make some other arrangement. But in the meantime, let's get together to solve the problem of where to put things."

One's natural inclination might be to say, "Why are you always speaking *loshon hora* (malicious gossip) on the phone? Don't you have a minimum commitment to Torah?" But it would be much more effective to say, "I find it hard to keep the laws of *loshon hora* without constant review. Would you like to set a time to study them together?"

Criticism should not be directed at the person but at the issues. The husband should withhold judgment about his wife's culpability. Instead of commenting on what she "always" does, he should rather address the problem at hand. Also, he should be careful to express an awareness of the difficulty anyone faces in avoiding whatever he is criticizing her for. In addition, he should always try to include himself in the problem to avoid the implication that he considers her inferior because of her fault. In a word, proper criticism should communicate the message that he cares for her despite the particular problem.

Although the Sages say that whoever does not protest against sins committed in his household is caught up in the punishment for those sins,[8] the Talmud also says in that same tractate that one must nevertheless be careful to reprimand a wife gently — otherwise, this will cause more sins than it will prevent.[9]

Although the Torah commands us to reprimand our erring fellow Jew,[10] one who cannot do so without hurting the other person's feelings is free of this obligation.[11]

From a practical as well as a halachic standpoint, harsh criticism ought to be avoided. Gentle speech is the most effective way to get one's point across. When the Torah was given at Sinai, it was communicated in a more gentle manner to women than to men. God told Moshe to address men in the form of *vesageyd*, i.e., "words as hard as sinews [*giddin*]". To the women he was ordered to speak in the form of *vesomar* —soft language.[12] "Words as hard as sinews" turn women off — even when the words of God are being spoken. The message gets across only when spoken in a warm, friendly way.

Rather than improving his wife, a husband risks poisoning his marriage through harsh criticism. If a woman feels that she is unloved, she responds by bickering and nagging. This is why, more often than not, nagging by a wife means that her husband is not paying her enough attention.

Woman's Ego

Criticizing a wife harshly is unnecessary for another reason: a women's ego is not as demanding as a man's. Men naturally balk at following someone else's ideas; they prefer to be first and to have others follow them. Women generally do not suffer from these emotional problems.

A man will rarely agree to marry a woman taller than he. Looking up to another person, especially a wife, goes against his masculine nature. Also, he is likely to be terrified by a powerful woman whom he perceives to be a threat to his masculinity. On the other hand, a woman will generally insist on marrying a taller and stronger man. Not only does her female ego accept this, but on the contrary, she will generally seek out a man whom she can admire, respect, and look up to as they journey through life together. By her nature a woman expresses her love and derives satisfaction by devoting herself to the man whom she loves.[13]

All of this, it should be emphasized, is true provided that a woman is convinced that her husband cares for her. A woman feels cheated if she has to serve a man for whom she has no love or respect or who she feels does not love her.

In fact, this may partially explain the rise of the

women's liberation movement. Women quite accurately sensed that men — to whom they naturally looked for leadership — were selfish, caring not for the women around them but primarily for their own pleasures and needs. They refused to be used by men whom they could not respect, and rebelled in anger against their domination. This very reason, incidentally, explains why this movement has never seriously affected homes where Torah is the paramount value. A woman is ready to subordinate herself to a husband who joins her in working together towards unselfish goals, such as Torah learning, spiritual growth, and building a Jewish family.

Woman's Spiritual Sensitivity

Women have a greater natural orientation towards spirituality than men, which is why the Sages say that the reward promised women in the world-to-come is greater than that promised to men.[14] This is why women, unlike their husbands, did not succumb to the temptation of worshipping the Golden Calf.[15] And the Torah was given first to women and only afterwards to men because they are more zealous in performing mitzvos.[16]

The converse is also true: men are innately more disposed to doing evil than women, and are more obsessed with their lusts and desires. Men, not women, spend lifetimes struggling for power and wealth; murders of passion are generally a male occupation.

Because of her spiritual sensitivity and more temperate drives and passions, women have a keener sense for judging situations and individuals. Classically, it has always been women in Jewish history who have warded off disaster through this insight. Sarah demanded that Yishmael be driven away because she noticed in him evil qualities which posed a threat to her son Yitzchak's spiritual development.[17] Rivka saw Eysav's true wicked nature even while her husband, Yitzchak, was planning to give him his blessings.[18] The wife of On ben Peles kept her husband from deluding himself into following Korach on a path to sure destruction.[19] Avigail knew how to convince King David to keep from taking sword in an improper battle.[20] The Sages say that a woman has deeper insight into even a guest's character[21]; it goes without saying, therefore, that she recognizes the true character of the husband with whom she constantly lives. Thus, a wise husband, aware of his wife's heightened sense of perception, will understand that it is mandatory for him to deal with his wife with utter honesty in all facets of life — religious, spiritual, and material.

NOTES TO CHAPTER FIVE

1. Chazon Ish, in letter cited in note No. 1 to Chap. 4. Women's greater dependency on others has also been scientifically documented, as in *Encyclopedia Brittanica*, Vol. 27, p. 319b.
2. Above-cited letter.
3. Letter by Rav Yaakov Kaniefsky ("The Steipeler") ז״ל, renowned Torah great. Copy with author.
4. *Kiddushin 7A.*
5. Warren and Baller, *Bedwetting: Origins and Treatments*, Pergammon Press, 1975.
6. *Shabbos 113a.*
7. *Pesachim 109a.*

8. *Shabbos 54b.*
9. *Ib. 34a.*
10. *Vayikra 19:17.*
11. Rav Chayim of Volozhin, *Keser Rosh*, No. 143, printed in *Siddur Ishey Yisrael (Siddur HaGra).*
12. *Mechilta* to *Shemos 19:3*, cited in *Rashi ad loc.*
13. See *Bechoros 30b.*
14. *Berachos 17a.*
15. *Tur, Orach Chayim 417*, citing *Pirkey de-Rabbi Eliezer.*
16. *Shemos Rabba 28, 2.*
17. *Bereyshis 21, 9.*
18. *Bereyshis, Chap. 27.*
19. *Bemidbar Rabba 18, 15.*
20. *Shmuel I, Chap. 25.*
21. *Berachos 10a.*

6

MORE ON THE FEMALE NATURE
Emotional Sensitivity

A woman's superior emotional sensitivity hardly needs to be demonstrated. She is the one who will shriek with joy over good news, and she is the one who will be drying her tears at a funeral. The Sages clearly recognize this. They observe that "נשים רחמניות הן" — "Women are merciful,"[1] and, referring to a woman's lifelong capacity for joy, the Sages say that "a six year old girl and a sixty year old woman will both dance similarly to the sound of music."[2] That the word, *rachamim*-mercy, is related to the word, *rechem*-womb, suggests that heightened, emotional sensitivity is bound up with the maternal instinct.

Because women are more emotionally sensitive than men, men are commanded to be especially careful not to hurt their feelings. As the Sages say:

לעולם יהא אדם זהיר באונאת אשתו
שמתוך שדמעתה מצויה אונאתה קרובה

— "One should always be careful not to hurt his wife, for just as her tears flow more readily, she is hurt more readily."[3] This means to say that a woman does not cry more readily over a slight to her honor because she reacts over-emotionally. On the contrary, the threshold of pain which brings her to tears is the same as that of a man. But she cries more readily because she experiences more pain than a man from the same abuse. For a man, only massive abuse can generate an emotional pain severe enough to cause him to cry. It follows, therefore, that any woman who is offended to the point that she breaks out in tears is undergoing this same degree of suffering no matter how slight this offense might be by masculine standards.

Often men are prone to say: "My wife is so sensitive; she cries over the silliest things." Translated, this means: "It is not my fault that she is hurt so easily; if she feels like indulging in crying this is her problem." From the above-cited comment of the Sages we see that this response is wrong. If a woman is "overly" sensitive this is because she is overly hurt. Given this fact of life, a husband would be foolish to make light of his wife's tears — and downright callous to bring them on.

Thought Processes

Despite the claims of more militant wings of feminism, there are definite, clear-cut, and ultimately innate differences between the ways in which males and females use their minds. Research has shown that men do better than women in spatial visualization (for example, in drawing a mental diagonal to a mental image of a square) and thus are superior in tasks requiring spatial orientation and mechanical comprehension.[4] In practical terms this means that a woman is more likely than a man to find it difficult to follow a map — or even to give street directions accurately. On the other hand, women are better than men in verbal skills, such as recognizing, comprehending, and remembering words.[4] This has been recognized to have a physiological basis,[5] since spatial visualization is related to the right brain hemisphere. Men, researchers believe, use their right hemisphere to process information while women use their left.[6] (Scholars knowledgeable in Kabbalah studies have pointed out that it is a standard element of the Sages' teachings that the right hemisphere of the brain is related to male cognition as well as to the visual faculties, while the left hemisphere is related to female cognition as well as to the auditory faculties.)

There is another well-recognized difference between men and women although the reason for this is less clear. This is that women are not as successful as men in mathematics, and, when given the choice, are less likely than men to choose courses related to this subject.[7] It is common knowledge that there is a very small percentage of women, compared to men, majoring in abstract mathematics in universities.

There are two major clichés offered as explanations for this phenomenon: women lack the mental ability required by mathematics; and that society steers women away from fields like mathematics. Neither of these is accurate.

All analyses of the elements which are thought to contribute to skill in cognition indicate that there is no significant difference between the sexes.[8] One leading scholar suggests that the phenomenon is a product of men's superior spatial visualization skills, arguing that women who solve mathematical problems verbally (as many mathematicians do) should be just as successful.[8] But this researcher does not make clear how success in mathematics is related to visualization, or why, in the final analysis, women do not score as high as men do on mathematics tests.

It is just as difficult to explain away this disparity by invoking social pressures which make careers in mathematics unattractive to women. There are just as many such pressures militating against careers in law, engineering and medicine, which fields have a much larger proportion of women than mathematics.

My understanding of the Sages leads me to believe that the missing element is not a difference in intellectual skills *per se* but in a difference in innate motivation.[9] Women simply have less interest than men in matters which have no practical application. Mathematics is more removed from actual application to real-life situations than other subjects, and consequently women are not as attracted to its study, nor are they as motivated to master it. On the other hand, men, because they are not as application-oriented are more attracted to abstract concepts.

One of the areas in which this difference between men and women is most evident is in the study of Talmud. More so than in mathematics, most of Talmudic study involves topics and issues which are not immediately, if at all, applicable to everyday life. Although ultimately this study enables a student to apply Halacha to real-life situations, it is only after he invests years of full-time grappling with non-practical issues that he learns the Talmudic methodology and theory which makes this possible. Women who have become involved in Talmudic study generally find this at best unrewarding, and at worst boring: they tend to find it difficult to maintain the motivation to invest so much time in such an abstract occupation. A woman has an affinity to those areas of Torah study which affect real-life behavior and situations, rather than those areas which are primarily abstract.

This idea in itself could explain why women are exempt from the mitzvah of studying Torah. Without the natural motivation for understanding the theoretical, which becomes the catalyst for full-time and life-long dedication which Torah scholarship demands, there exists the possibility that the depths of the laws will be improperly understood and that inaccurate readings and interpretations of the law will result. Not the absence of intellectual ability, but the absence of a natural bent for theoretical abstractions exempts women from this study.

Recognition of the fact that men and women have different thought patterns will often enable husband and wife to be more tolerant of each other. Occasionally, men or women grow irritated with each other's reasoning or approach to problem solving. A woman's way of organizing her home, her daily schedule — or even her personal telephone list — can be a source of exasperation for a man. Also, joint study by husband and wife of theoretical Torah subjects is often unsatisfying for the same reason. Appreciating the fact that there is a male and female way of thinking will help allay these sources of annoyance.

While men might not use the same method of thinking as their wives, they should appreciate that women have superior talent and efficiency in dealing with everyday life. The Sages say that one should always consult his wife in decisions dealing with "matters of this world".[10] Women's unique intelligence gives them more efficient tools than men for the realistic, hands-on management of everyday crises. One reason is that a woman is more practically oriented and therefore is not as easily attracted by flights of fantasy. Another reason is that she is able to foresee the ultimate effects of any situation better than a man,[11] and this makes her capable of insights which can often protect her family from unwise decisions.

The difference between male and female thought processes, like all other differences between them, have been put there for very good reasons. They are deserved of being mutually respected, not denigrated.

"Daatan Kalos"

The Sages say of women: *"daatan kalos,"*[12] i.e., their *daas*, a particular aspect of intelligence, is "light." What the Sages meant by this is often misinterpreted. They certainly did not mean to say that women are less intelligent than men. On the contrary, the Sages teach us that women have more *bina*, another quality of intelligence, than men.[13] There is even a passage in the Talmud which refers to a wise woman (a *chachomo*) as possessing this "light" quality of *daas*[14] — an inherent contradiction if it refers to lack of intelligence. What, then, is this mental quality called *daas*, and what about the fact that women possess it in a "lighter" form?

From the Sages' application of this principle, it would seem that it means that women have a capacity to move from one activity or idea to another with more ease than men,[15] while men tend to be more focused upon, and involved in, a single, specific idea or activity which interests them. Concentration and involvement are a function of the aspect of intelligence called *daas*. Women's "lighter" *daas* means that their *daas* can more easily move from one area of concentration to another, just as a lighter object can be moved more easily than a heavy one.

This principle finds expression in the statement of the Sages that relocating from one house to another is more painful for a man than for a woman.[16] Because of their "lighter" *daas* women adjust more easily.

Women were probably endowed with this quality in order to facilitate the building and nurturing of the home and family. Maintaining a home and raising children is multi-faceted work, requiring great mental and emotional agility. With a *daas* which is much more flexible than men's, which does not suffer as much as men's from interruptions, and which makes it easier to juggle various obligations simultaneously, women are well endowed for managing a busy household. At least one expert has said, in fact, that this talent gives women an advantage in being business administrators.[17] A man, on the other hand, can be driven to near madness by the constant interruptions, distractions, and incompleted work of a woman's normal routine. Any man who has ever experienced taking over the duties of a household for a day can testify to this.

I know of a man who decided to offer his services to his wife one Erev Shabbos, announcing that he was ready to perform any duty she requested. During the following hour he was asked to: hold the baby; put down the baby to turn off the stove; bring the mop; turn on the stove; pick up the baby; turn off the stove; put away the baby and start peeling potatoes; stop peeling potatoes to calm the baby's crying; start peeling again; empty the garbage pail which was overflowing with peelings; put down the pail to pick up the baby who had begun crying; clean up the mess caused by his inadvertent overturning of the pail as he picked the baby up; turn on the stove again — until he was close to mental collapse. He finally decided he could take it no longer and in an obviously tense voice told his wife that he was leaving the house. His wife could not understand why he was suddenly leaving when she needed him most, and why he had become so upset over having to help her for just an hour.

Incidentally, this helps us understand the reason why Pharoah ordered his male slaves to do women's labors, and female slaves to do men's labors:[18] this was a scheme devised to inflict maximum torture on both sexes. Women doing men's work was physical torture since they simply lacked the strength for it. And men doing women's labor was mental torture, since men lacked the emotional strength for it.

There is another aspect of women's greater capacity

for adjustment. For example, if a man is interrupted by a telephone call after having begun a certain task, he will be more likely than a woman to return to it after the call. His "heavier" *daas* does not permit him to sever his attachment to his original activity even after he becomes involved with his second occupation. But a woman, once she gets involved in the new activity, is more likely to lose track of what she was originally doing. Her "lighter" *daas* has become detached from the first endeavor and is now concentrated fully upon the second. In Hebrew, "losing track" of an activity is called *"heseyach hadaas,"* or removal of *daas*. Again, *daas* is that intellectual quality which enables a person to fasten himself to a particular activity.

Perhaps this accounts for the general observation — almost a cliché — that woman have more difficulty with promptness than men. This may be because of their "lighter" *daas*. They may have scheduled their day a certain way, but because they are easily drawn into fresh activities, they may deviate from their schedule. Lateness, especially on Erev Shabbos, is often a source of marital strife. But if men would recognize that such lateness could very well stem from the special kind of *daas* with which women were endowed, they might react more calmly.

Her Home

While a man, especially during the first years of marriage, looks at his home as a dormitory, a woman sees it as an extension of herself; it represents her personhood. Rav Chayim Shmuelevitz זצ״ל[19] used to say that the enjoyment he used to get from compliments on his *shiyurim* (lectures on Talmud) taught him to be careful to compliment his wife on her accomplishments in the home. His wife's Shabbos meal, he used to say, is her equivalent to his *shiyur*. Indeed, every aspect of the home — how it is decorated, how it is organized and what impression it makes — is an expression of his wife as homemaker.

A woman is therefore more sensitive to the appearance of her home than a man is. She suffers greatly if her home is not neat and presentable. A husband, for example, cannot understand why a wife gets so upset because he has left his socks on the floor. To a woman, however, this is nearly the same as if he would have left his socks hanging on the front doorknob. She sees his sloppiness reflecting on her.

I know of a family which was once desperately trying to sell its home. After some time, a buyer finally presented himself. He was leaving town, but the description of the house seemed to make it exactly what he was looking for. He was ready to sign a contract provided that he could inspect the house within the hour.

Although some sixty thousand dollars was at stake, the lady of the house refused him permission to look it over. Her reason: she was ashamed to let him see it before she had a chance to straighten up. As a result, the deal fell through.

Very few men would react this way. Still, no man has a right to get angry with his wife for such a reaction, since he cannot gauge the degree of humiliation she would experience by showing a house in disarray.

Bearing this in mind, it goes without saying that if a difference of opinion should ever arise over how to decorate or arrange a house, a man should always yield to his wife since these are issues of greater personal significance to her.

The difference in priorities may become a clash if a man overlooks this reality. Consider a common enough scenario:

Erev Shabbos (when it is common to have all sorts of arguments) there is no time to do everything before Shabbos comes in. A quarrel develops over whether washing the floors should come before taking a shower.

To the husband the answer is obvious. Washing one's body for Shabbos is a religious obligation; there is no such requirement for washing floors. But few women would agree. A house in disarray, a dirty floor when guests arrive, can be painfully embarrassing. From her perspective she has a powerful point. The husband will quarrel with her over this only because he does not understand her perspective.

Physical Differences

Men are often unaware or insufficiently conscious of physical differences between men and women. For instance, because women have only 55% of the muscular strength of men and 65% of the stamina,[20] they tire more easily. Medical opinion has it that women also need, on the average, one more hour of sleep than men need.[21]

Most important are the far-reaching effects of menstruation and pregnancy. These effects prompted the comment by a noted gynecologist that every groom should realize that he is marrying three women: normal, menstruous, and pregnant.[22]

A woman undergoes a profound change in her metabolism once a month. The physical changes cause various degrees of emotional stress. A woman is more likely to become shrill, annoyed, aggressive, and impatient with her husband during this time. She is usually tense — far from the calm, relaxed woman the husband thought he was marrying.

Instead of taking this sudden change in moods as a personal affront, a husband should understand its hormonal source. He should realize that just as his wife has become physically separated from him during this time, she has become emotionally separated as well.

Although the Halacha forbids using expressions of endearment during this period,[23] one should be sensitive to her feelings of being rejected. A woman is terrified by a husband who is warm one day and cold the next. One has to make additional efforts to be considerate, kind and thoughtful during this time. A woman is likely to interpret any harsh words from her husband as a sign that he does not love her. Although his harshness may be in response to her own shrillness, she may nonetheless conclude from this that he only cares about her as long as she can provide him with physical gratification. Giving a woman such a feeling, as we have noted above in the name of a great sage, is akin to spilling her blood.

The *harchaka*/separation requirements[24] during this period are vital for the observance of the *niddah* laws. Reflecting marvelous psychological insights, the former are designed to remind the couple of the prohibitions against intimate contact between them. If, however, a coldness accompanies their observance, this will be perceived as reflecting a lack of love — which can be extremely painful to a woman. Therefore, it is especially important to be careful about acting in a manner which might be construed as a lack of love while a wife is menstruous. This is especially true during the early months of marriage when a misunderstanding of this nature can cause serious damage.

Pregnancy

During pregnancy, a woman undergoes even more dramatic changes. This should not be surprising. If a man could experience what it is like to have a baby growing inside his body, he would, in all likelihood, be more understanding.

The physical changes often include, for the first three months, nausea and an inability to eat many foods, such as meat. A pregnant woman needs more sleep than usual, is generally sluggish, and often feels "low." Besides suffering a loss of appetite for food, she often loses, as well, her appetite for marital relations.

Perhaps more important are the emotional changes which take place in a woman during pregnancy. Foremost, she is sensitive to becoming less attractive. It may appear odd that this is what concerns her, but if one considers that a woman's personal appearance is profoundly important to her,[25] one will understand why this is often one of the first thoughts which enters a young woman's mind when she discovers that she is expecting a child.

At the same time — and nearly to the same degree — she may become extremely anxious about the welfare of her unborn baby. Often a husband who is thrilled by the news that his wife is pregnant cannot understand why she does not share his enthusiasm. But a common worry of the mother — and rarely of a prospective father — is that her child may be born deformed.

A husband's obligation, both under the general mitzvah of *chessed* and under his specific responsibility as a husband, is to recognize what his wife is undergoing and to ease as much of her physical and emotional discomfort as he can. This requires a good deal of sensitivity and sympathy.

Motherhood

A baby's life depends on its mother, and a mother is well aware of this. A mother, especially a new mother, is more likely to be concerned about a baby's health than will be her husband. She may worry and want to rush out to a doctor at the slightest suspicion that something is wrong.

Occasionally, a husband will react angrily to a wife's over-zealous care of the baby. This stems, in part, from the the fact that his wife showers more attention on the baby than on him. In addition, he responds to his wife's unwillingness to follow his opinion in matters affecting the baby as a personal affront. Of course, this response is absurd.

A woman was given the maternal instinct in order that she care for her children. This instinct is responsible for the emotional pain she suffers whenever her child's welfare is threatened. A physiological stimulus of this maternal instinct has even been identified: a baby's cry releases the hormone oxytocin in a mother's body which causes her discomfort until the needs of her baby are taken care of.[26] It is physically impossible for a mother to ignore this stimulus.

For a husband to be affronted by his wife's reactions to a child's illness is therefore counterproductive. Surely no man would become jealous or angry when milk begins to flow in response to her sensing that her baby is hungry. Rather than argue over how sick the baby is, one should assume that her estimate of what needs to be done is probably the more accurate one. And one's efforts would better be directed towards helping soothe an already overwrought woman who hardly needs to contend with the additional problem of an agitated husband.

Individual Natures

Although we have noted many general characteristics of the female nature, it should be emphasized that no two women are the same. It is important for a husband to understand that his wife is an individual. He cannot reasonably expect her to act just as he would like her to, or just as his friends (or even books) have told him women act. An awareness of this will prevent much unnecessary criticism, with all its damaging ramifications.

Certain women, for example, like to sleep late; others are early risers. Some women feel fulfilled by household work; others prefer taking a job outside the house. Some women enjoy working with their hands, while others find that their hands are not so nimble.

Every woman has her own way of organizing her activities, her kitchen, and her home. Because, as we have noted, a woman looks at her home as an extension of her very being, her husband should respect her way of doing things.

A husband's recognition of his wife's natures, habits, and tastes is a small but mandatory contribution towards making domestic life mutually pleasant.

NOTES TO CHAPTER SIX

1. *Megillah 14b.*
2. *Mo'ed Katan 9b.*
3. *Bava Metzia 59a;* cf. *Kesubos 67b: "Boshta shel isha meruba mishel ish."*
4. MacCoby and Jacklin, *The Psychology of Sex Differences*, pp. 85-89 Stanford University Press, 1966; Flanagan *et al.,* (Project Talent) Palo Alto, Cal., 1961.
5. "Further Evidence of Sex-Linked Major-Gene Influence on Human Spatial Visualizing Ability," *American Journal of Human Genetics 25* (January 1973).
6. "Sex and the Single Hemisphere: Specialization of the Right Hemisphere for Spatial Process," *Science* 193 pp. 425-7.
7. MacCoby and Jacklin, *op. cit.*; Flanagan *et al., op. cit.*
8. MacCoby and Jacklin, *op. cit.*
9. *Yoma 66b.*
10. *Bava Metzia 59a.*
11. *Niddah 45b:* "A woman has more *binah* than a man." *"Binah"* refers to the faculty of foreseeing developments.
12. *Shabbos 33b.*
13. *Niddah 45b.*
14. *Pesachim 88b* and *Rashi ib.*
15. *Shabbos ib.; Kiddushin 80b.*
16. *Sanhedrin 26a.*
17. Presidential advisor on employment, cited in "Managing the Woman's Way," *Newsweek,* March 17, 1986.
18. *Sota 11b.*
19. World renowned scholar and Rosh HaYeshivah of Mirrer Yeshiva, Jerusalem; d. 5740/1980
20. Pentagon Study, cited in *Newsweek,* Nov. 11, 1985.
21. Isselbacher, *et al., Harrison's Principles of Internal Medicine, 9th Edition,* p.127, McGraw Hill, 1980.
22. Dick-Read, *Childbirth Without Fear,* Harper and Row, 1972.
23. *Yoreh Deah 195;* these are subtle reminders that intimate contact between them during the menstrual, or *niddah,* period is forbidden.
24. *Ib.*
25. See Chap. 5.
26. Levin, "The Feminist Mystique," citing work by John Money and a large body of physiologists, *Commentary,* December, 1980.

7

HILLEL AND THE CAUSES OF ANGER

Marriage would not be so challenging if only the problems we have discussed were involved — i.e., maintaining civility, observing the interpersonal mitzvos, and coming to terms with a wife's nature. A more serious problem, however, faces every married couple: anger. More than anything else, it is anger which undermines the relationship between husband and wife.

Anger can be expressed in many forms. While it is usually conveyed through a raised and threatening voice, it can also express itself in the mild form of annoyance or through sarcasm and insult. If one wants peace in his home he has to learn to avoid, or at least to control, all forms of anger.

Before discussing how to deal with anger, we must pinpoint its causes; namely, what provokes anger and which circumstances make it difficult to control.

Fortunately for us, the Sages have taught us what

these causes are in the well-known story of Hillel and the
man who tried to anger him:[1]

> Two men made a wager with each other. "Whoever can
> make Hillel angry," they said, "will get 400 *zuz*."
>
> ...That day it was Erev Shabbos, and Hillel was washing
> his hair. One of the men passed by the entrance to Hillel's
> house. He yelled out: "Who here is called Hillel? Who
> here is called Hillel?"
>
> Hillel wrapped himself in his cloak and went out to him.
> "My son," the sage said, "what is it that you want?"
>
> "I have a question to ask," the man began.
>
> "Ask, my son, ask," Hillel responded.
>
> "Why is it that the heads of the Babylonians are round?"
>
> "You have asked a very important question," Hillel
> answered. "Because they do not have alert midwives."
>
> The man waited a short while until Hillel had gone back to
> his bath. Then he yelled out again: "Who here is called
> Hillel? Who here is called Hillel?"
>
> Hillel wrapped himself in his cloak and went out to him.
> He said to him: "My son," he said, "what is it you wish?"
>
> "I have a question to ask," the man said again.
>
> And again Hillel encouraged him: "Ask, my son, ask."
>
> "Why are the eyes of the Tarmudians weak?"
>
> And again Hillel answered: "You have asked a very
> important question. Because they live among sand
> dunes."
>
> The man went away, waited a short while, returned, and
> yelled out a third time: "Who here is called Hillel?"
>
> Hillel wrapped himself in his cloak and went out to him.
> He asked him: "My son, what is it you wish?"

Once again the man repeated: "I have a question to ask."

"Ask, my son, ask," came the patient response.

"Why are the feet of the Africans broad?"

"My son, you have asked a very important question. Because they live among the swamps."

Frustrated, the man made one final attempt: "I have many questions to ask but I am afraid that you might become angry."

Hillel calmly sat down before him. "Ask all the questions that you would ask," the sage offered.

In desperation, the man asked: "Are you Hillel who is called leader of the Jewish people?"

"Yes."

"If you are he, then may there be no more like you in Israel!"

"Why, my son, why?"

"Because I have lost 400 *zuz* through you."

"Control yourself," said Hillel, concluding the exchange. "It is better that you lose twice four hundred *zuz* through Hillel than that Hillel become angry."

All the methods which the man used to anger Hillel derive from his understanding of one important principle: that anger is nothing more than the ultimate expression of *gaavah* — pride.[2] The Sages refer to the evil inclination towards anger as a false god within a man.[3] This false god is actually the god of self-worship. We become angry when our exaggerated self-esteem is threatened.

When threatened, we wish, deep in our subconscious, to destroy whoever threatens us. However, because of our convictions or our upbringing we are unwilling or unable to do so, and we control ourselves. The result is subdued violence, i.e., anger. The loud voice of anger implicitly threatens to harm the person who is challenging our pride. The verbal violence we direct at him is intended to destroy his worth. All of this we do to avenge our beleaguered pride.

The man who wanted to anger Hillel understood this principle well. In addition, he understood just as well which circumstances create the psychological pressures which make it difficult to control the reaction of anger. He therefore used a variety of techniques to arouse, to challenge, and to make it difficult for Hillel to contain, his feelings of affronted pride.

He began by calling out at the entrance of Hillel's house, "Who here is called Hillel?" By so doing, he demonstrated that Hillel, the most important person in the Jewish world, was a complete unknown to him; he wasn't even sure of his name and address. This affront to Hillel's self-esteem was meant to set the stage for the subsequent assault.

He waited until Erev Shabbos, the time of week when people are most busy. Because pressure makes it more difficult for one to control anger, Erev Shabbos was a perfect time to attempt to arouse it. He also waited until Hillel's hair was wet and going outdoors would be unpleasant for him — since discomfort makes it harder for one to control anger.

Finally, it is most difficult to control anger when

someone feels self-righteous. If he is interrupted while busy doing something which is clearly a mitzvah, he feels justi-fied in retaliating with anger, for he can tell himself that at stake is not merely his personal honor, but the honor of God, who commanded him to do the mitzvah. In this case, his moral training does not obligate him to control himself, and his inhibitions fall by the wayside. Thus the man waited until Hillel was engaged in the mitzvah of preparing for Shabbos when he would be most vulnerable.

Besides interrupting a very important person; besides interrupting the performance of a mitzvah; besides inter-rupting at the least opportune time of the week — each in itself a sufficient provocation to anger for most people — the would-be instigator interrupted for ridiculous matters which never should have been brought up at all.

The causes of anger are cumulative: the more an affront is repeated the more difficult it becomes to control anger. Not only does the victim wish to retaliate for the present affront, he also wants to take revenge for past offenses. In addition, a repeated affront becomes more grievous with each repetition. The first, or even the second time, one may want to assume the offense to have been unintentional. But by the third interruption, one could be certain that he was the target of deliberate abuse. Yet, Hillel remained calm and patient.

When all else failed, the man decided to take another approach: to insult Hillel directly.

He prepared him for the insult by attempting to lessen Hillel's motivation for control: "I have many questions to ask but I am afraid you will become angry." In so saying, he acknowledged Hillel's moral right to get angry with him. Then he tried to build up Hillel's feelings of self-importance. Whenever someone is made to feel important he is more sensitive to a subsequent insult, as it is written, "Pride comes before the fall."[4] The man therefore asked Hillel, "Are you Hillel, leader of the Jewish people?" When Hillel answered, "Yes," he unleashed what he believed would be his decisive blow: "Then may there be no more like you in Israel!"

But this, too, failed to anger the sage. Because anger arises out of one's perception that one's prestige is under attack, this had no effect on Hillel. Hillel was so humble that he perceived himself unworthy of honor. He had no pride which could be attacked.

It appears from Hillel's comment, "Control yourself," that the man who tried to anger Hillel became angry himself. This is not surprising. His pride was now shattered, having lost the wager and a sizable sum of money besides. And he blamed his failure on Hillel. But the losses, as Hillel explained to him, were not a legitimate basis for anger since there is nothing more valuable than controlling anger. Anger may be a short-term way of gaining satisfaction, but it is worthless in comparison to the eternal value of maintaining self-control.

To summarize, the principles derived from this story are: a) anger is a reaction to injured pride; b) discomfort and pressure make it difficult to control anger; c) feelings of self-righteousness weaken the desire for control; d) it becomes more difficult to control anger each time the affront is repeated.

In the next two chapters we shall attempt to apply these principles.

NOTES TO CHAPTER SEVEN

1. *Shabbos 30b-31a.*
2. Vilna Gaon, *Beur al kama agados*, section beginning "בין גלא".
3. *Shabbos 105b.*
4. *Mishley 16:18.*

8

AFFRONTS, REAL AND IMAGINED

We tend to react with anger or annoyance (low-grade anger) when our ego is affronted. [1] In order to combat and contain these destructive reactions, we must become conscious of the variety of affronts which can trigger them, such as criticism, jealousy, and disobedience.

Criticism

All criticism is taken as a personal attack. Criticism implies that we have a fault or, at least, that we are not fully perfect. Many of us live in the illusion that we are nearly faultless. Although we are all sometimes forced to recognize that we have certain deficiencies (when, for example, we are confronted with people of superior intelligence or character), we tell ourselves that we are not interested in being better, or that we have not been blessed with the same opportunities. Anyone who criticizes us is, in effect, claiming that we are really not as faultless as we had imagined. And this is taken as an insult.

Of course, not everyone thinks of himself so highly.

But even people with a low self-image are no less offended when another person points out their faults. Because they have become accustomed to living with the illusion that no one notices their shortcomings, an intimation to the contrary is also taken as a personal affront. Regardless of their self-image, people's response to criticism is generally the same: anger.

This is especially so with respect to criticism offered by a wife. Unless his ego is controlled, a husband usually expects his wife to admire and adore him constantly. As a wise person once said, "The average man wants his wife to be smart enough to understand him and stupid enough to appreciate him." If it is true that criticism generally evokes anger, it is doubly true in the case of a wife's criticism. A critical wife, in most men's perceptions, is failing to perform her wifely duty; consequently, this compounds their angry response.

There are two standard responses to criticism, both designed to strengthen the ego — and therefore the anger: a) justification, and b) counterattack. Both are totally incorrect. Justification means saying, in effect: "I am right and you are wrong." Counterattack means: "I am wrong but you are, too," or, "two wrongs make a right."

Consider the following illustration: A wife asks her husband to buy some tomatoes on the way home from work. He forgets. When he arrives home she criticizes him for his forgetfulness. (If this has happened more than once she may even say, "You are *always* forgetting to do things I ask you to do.") In response to her criticism, the husband is likely to feel a sensation of anger welling up inside him.

If he chooses the justification response, a flood of excuses as to why he forgot the tomatoes will come to mind: "I wasn't feeling well today"; "Someone kept me busy and made me forget"; "I have too many things on my mind lately"; "I was in a rush"; *et al.* One cannot help but marvel at the human being's ability to think so quickly when under attack.

The counterattack response sounds like this: "True, I forgot, but last week you forgot something more important"; "You are always asking me to do things which you can take care of yourself; don't you know how busy I am?"; "Even when I get you tomatoes you leave half of them rotting in the vegetable bin"; "I may have forgotten, but this is nothing compared to how wrong it is to get upset with me for this."

Both of these types of responses are misguided. They result in charges and countercharges which lead only to strife.

There is only one correct response: an honest appraisal of the charge. Very often the criticism is accurate. If so, even if the criticism is offered the wrong way, the reaction should simply be: "I am wrong." One might even add, "Thank you for bringing this to my attention." This will defuse the tension and will bring the whole affair to an end. The Sages say, "If someone calls you 'donkey,' put a saddle on your back."[2] The Vilna Gaon tells us that this means: If someone says you have a fault, admit it and he will stop talking about it.[3] This is a proven method which will prevent the inevitable quarreling which the first two responses engender.

It is possible, of course, that after an honest appraisal of the criticism, the charge will have been found to have been false. Does this give a person good reason to become angry?

The answer is unequivocally negative; even this is no reason for anger. More often than not, baseless criticism is due to a misunderstanding. Why else would a wife deliberately offer false criticism? A misunderstanding is, of course, no reason for anger. If the husband would think instead of reacting instinctively, he would most probably be able to identify the source of the misunderstanding.

If, finally, there is no basis in fact — or in error — for the criticism, and a true and inexcusable insult has been hurled at the husband, this is still not a reason for anger. Firstly, anger is forbidden;[4] it is an urge which has to be controlled. Secondly, as explained below, anger is a futile and counter-productive response in any situation. If one does feel anger beginning to brew within, the only sensible response is to control it in some way, the best being total silence. (Controlling anger will be discussed in detail in Chapter Nine.)

Jealousy

Because of our inflated view of ourselves, we often cannot tolerate the better treatment — or even the praise — given to someone else. This is anger triggered by jealousy, which is also bound up with injured pride. Why, we think to ourselves, does so-and-so deserve good treatment or praise but not I? Obviously, the omission means that we are not regarded as highly as the other person.

We will be especially hurt if so-and-so is in competition with us. Competition makes us more sensitive to the success of our rival; it makes us more aware of our own failure. The Sages say that every tradesman dislikes every other tradesman in his field.[5] Each tradesman feels that if not for his competitors everyone would recognize that he is the best. The success of the competitor is taken as an affront to his own prestige.

Very often a husband is jealous of his wife's love for her parents. For this reason, if a wife praises her parents in front of him, he will find himself growing annoyed or angry with her. Such a reaction is all the more likely if a wife praises another man before her husband.

Remarkably enough, a person may even be jealous of his own child. If, for example, he feels that his wife pays more attention to their infant than to him, he will find himself angry both at his wife and the baby.

Jealousy can often be counteracted by the simple admission that jealousy exists. Facing the immaturity of the emotion lets in a healthy gust of air.

To counteract jealousy, one might very profitably try to awaken in oneself feelings of love for the object of the jealousy. This can be accomplished by reminding oneself of all the good which the person in question has done for him, or of all his desirable qualities. Love makes the lover desire to benefit his beloved. Where this feeling exists, there can be no place for jealousy, an emotion which arouses a desire to take something away from the object of the jealousy.

Awakening love is effective not only in counteracting jealousy but against all types of anger, as noted in the next chapter. Since becoming angry at anyone means, in effect, that one would subconsciously like to get rid of him (as explained in the previous chapter), evoking emotions of love towards him will neutralize both this desire and the anger itself.

Disobedience

We are all hurt if our wishes are not carried out. In our all-consuming selfishness, we must have all our desires fulfilled. Anyone who frustrates these desires is, by definition, our enemy.

This certainly holds true for a wife. We have already discussed how men enter marriage fantasizing about the imminent fulfillment of all their dreams and desires. Expecting to be kept always in good spirits, a husband who finds his desires even temporarily frustrated readily concludes that his wife has not been doing her job, or even that he should not have married her. Similarly, if a wife fails to carry out her husband's requests, a husband will treat her the same way he would treat someone who has failed to pay his debt on time, namely, with anger.

Even if the husband's requests are all being honored, an intimation that this will not continue in the future can bring about the same response of anger or annoyance. For example, a man asks his wife to stop off at the bank to make a deposit, but she forgets to do so. Were it a friend who forgot, he would feel no more than disappointment.

But since the wife did the forgetting, anger is the likely reaction.

Why is this so? Ordinarily, a husband who asks himself about his exaggerated reaction will probably explain that he "just cannot stand" unreliable people. But what really is at stake here is the husband's perception that his wife does not consider his wishes to be of supreme importance. He suspects that forgetting the bank deposit might be an indication that she does not see serving her husband as her primary duty. Therefore, his response, in the manner of all despots, is: "Off with her head!"

A husband's self-centeredness gives rise to anger when confronted with another form of disobedience: failure to accept his opinion or to follow his advice. It is always painful to have someone disagree with us. By not following our viewpoint he is, in effect, affronting our ego by communicating the message that he considers himself smarter than we are. Under ordinary circumstances, we may or may not react with anger, but if we believe that the person is obligated to heed us we will almost certainly react with anger.

Indeed, our anger is usually directly proportional to the degree to which we feel the other person is obligated to listen to us. Parents, for example, can get angry at a three-year-old for disobeying them. Unreasonably, the parents' honor is offended by the child's disobedience. After all, they told the child to eat and he refused to follow simple instructions. How dare he!

This is even truer with respect to older children.

Parents can become even violently angry with them for disobedience. This, in fact, is the explanation for child abuse. An older child's disobedience is interpreted as a gross personal insult. Because they have the intelligence to obey, they are expected to do so.

Following this reasoning, if a husband begins with the fantasy that his wife ought to adore and admire him without reservation, it is understandable that he will get angry or annoyed at her refusal to follow his opinion or to take his advice.

Quarrels often ensue when a man and wife are working together on a project (building a *sukkah*, for example). He will suggest a certain way of doing something; she will not agree. The husband feels his ego is at stake, and refuses to budge from his position. If the wife is just as adamant, the joint project will often end in joint anger.

Were marriage to be approached with Torah-oriented values, such anger could be avoided. In a Torah home there is no place for an argument. Rabbi Ada bar Ahava, the Talmudic figure, said that he merited long life because he never became upset with his wife over household matters.[6] We have said that a wife makes it possible for her husband to learn how to be kind to another human being. He must be concerned, therefore, about fulfilling her wishes, not about how unfulfilled are his own. Since a Jew should always be running away from pride and ego stimulation, he cannot possibly have a claim upon his wife to supply these to her husband. The idea that a wife must follow her husband blindly and adore him unconditionally is a dangerous delusion.

Angry demands for obedience are counterproductive: they make a wife less willing to listen to her husband. It is the nature of a woman to subordinate herself to her husband, but a woman will do so only if she feels her husband loves her. Anger creates the opposite impression and makes a woman want to rebel against her husband, to be rid of his domination.

In general, it is good advice for a husband to train himself not to overly rely upon his wife's services. In this way there will be less reason for him to be angry with her when they are not provided.

Anger over disobedience can be avoided if the situation is put into the proper perspective. Giving someone the benefit of a doubt is not only one of the 613 mitzvos of the Torah,[7] it is also good policy. If the wife forgets the husband's request that she go to the bank, this is not a sign of imminent mutiny. She may not have been able to do so. She may even have had to attend to other matters, quite possibly for the benefit of her husband and family. Any reasonable person would agree that it is extremely far-fetched to assume this to be rebellion against her husband's authority. The problem here is that the husband does not admit that rebellion is his worry. He just "cannot stand unreliable people."

Associations

Because of his past experiences, a husband may attach unintended significance to his wife's actions. Sometimes a wife can do an innocent or trivial act which will cause her husband great upset because of its associations.

For example, some husbands become very annoyed if their wives do not spell correctly. Lack of this skill to them means a lack of culture or intelligence. The husband looks at this as a personal affront. He is subconsciously afraid that she might demonstrate her ignorance in public and that, by association, he too will be branded uncultured and unintelligent.

I have known husbands who became annoyed if their wives opened up their eggs for them at breakfast. This reminded them, apparently, of some overbearing authority (such as an overprotective mother) in years gone by. The opened egg thereby became a symbol of an attempt at domination, and caused a "knee-jerk" reaction of annoyance and anger.

Sometimes the way a woman dresses will upset a husband because of the disagreeable associations which the style engenders. Even squeezing a toothpaste tube from the top can suggest an annoying wastefulness or lack of planning. These "loaded" behaviors can cause serious problems in relationships.

An engagement between a couple was nearly broken because the young woman occasionally would wrinkle her forehead. Even though the young man realized that his response was slightly irrational, he would become intolerably irritated whenever she would do this in his presence.

It did not take long to discover the source of his anger.

The young man's mother was a proper middle-class woman who believed that cultured people do not wrinkle their foreheads. From childhood she had admonished her son never to dare behave so boorishly. Naturally, as he grew up this became a symbol of boorishness for him. Furthermore, he was naturally horrified that his fiancée might wrinkle her forehead in his mother's presence, thus demonstrating her lack of culture.

Fortunately, the problem was not difficult to solve. As soon as he became aware of the reason behind his objections, the young man made peace with the wrinkles. Besides, when the girl learned about his objections, she began to control her wrinkling. The tragedy of a broken engagement was averted by putting an imagined affront into its proper "historical" perspective.

In the same manner, the annoying associations of a wife's innocent actions can be defused with honesty and self-awareness.

"The Principle of the Thing"

We often delude ourselves into thinking that we are angry for noble reasons. We will say, "I realize that what has happened is trivial. What bothers me is the principle of the thing."

A shopkeeper, for example, has overcharged you by seventy-five cents. You know this is not a large sum, but you are so upset that you toss and turn all night. Your extreme reaction, you tell yourself, is not due to the money involved but to the principle of dishonesty.

This analysis, however, is incorrect. It cannot be the principle of dishonesty which bothers you. Would you be as upset if the same thing had happened to your friend? And do you not complacently hear and read about all kinds of robberies regularly? The main reason for your distress is that the person who overcharged you has made you look stupid. The only "principle" involved is your firm belief that you are the cleverest person on earth.

The "principle of the thing" is not what it appears to be in the following illustration as well. A man has arranged to meet his wife at a certain street corner at ten A.M. sharp. She arrives forty-five minutes late, by which time the husband is fuming. No explanation by the wife can placate him. The husband is aware that he is overreacting to her lateness. He understands that accidents can happen, and he made good use of his waiting time mentally reviewing some important ideas. Still, he cannot contain his anger. He explains his extreme reaction by telling himself that he cannot tolerate another person not keeping his word.

It may well be, however, that he interprets her lateness as an act of disrespect toward him. He reminds himself of the times she rushed herself to keep appointments with doctors, with teachers, and with lawyers. Her lateness means that she does not consider him as important as these other people. He is angry because, in his perception of the situation, she has slighted him. By admitting that our ego has been offended, it will be much easier to contain the anger.

Retaliation for Past Grievances

As we have seen from the story of Hillel, the causes of anger can be cumulative. Even if we do not react to a stimulus for anger, it remains in our memory. And if the offense is repeated we become doubly angry. Also, as we have noted, the more an offense is repeated, the more we feel it is being done deliberately — and the more it angers us. Consequently, whenever a person senses that his anger is out of proportion to the apparent cause, he would be well-advised to consider whether he is taking revenge for past grievances.

For example, a wife leaves to go shopping and, forgetting that her husband had previously phoned her that he has no keys to the house, locks the door behind her. The husband returns, finds that he cannot enter the house and has to go somewhere else for an hour until his wife returns. Whether or not this brings him to anger, it registers in his mind as an act of thoughtlessness.

If, say, a week later, she forgets to give him a telephone message, he might become enraged. By itself, this second oversight would be considered trivial, but because something similar has happened before, he is convinced that her thoughtlessness is not an accident. "You are *always* doing these things to me," he declares, and a quarrel follows.

If a wife refuses to agree with her husband's viewpoint on a particular matter, and then she happens to dial a wrong number, the husband may react with a remark about her confused mind — actually referring to her unwillingness to accept his opinion in the earlier discussion.

If one day a husband asks his wife to prepare him an early supper and she forgets to do so, he will probably easily forgive her. But if she forgets her keys to the house a week later, he may comment, "Why are you always forgetting things?"

I once knew a couple on the verge of divorce whose story vividly illustrates the revenge motive. According to the husband, he wanted to end the marriage because he did not want to live with a woman who lacked a fundamental commitment to Torah. She, on the other hand, complained that she felt that he was unreasonably strict with her on religious matters.

The particular matter under dispute was his insistence that she refrain from using a certain type of salt shaker on Shabbos — and her refusal. One could get the impression from their quarrel that his wife simply did not share his zealous devotion to Halacha. Upon investigation, however, the true issues came out into the open.

Prior to the episode, the husband had a history of being embarrassed by his ignorance of fine details of the Shabbos laws (a very common cause of embarrassment, incidentally). Many times she had asked him, quite innocently, for the law for a particular situation, and he was forced to respond that he did not know. This proved especially embarrassing when guests were present. On several occasions, he had even given her the wrong ruling, which she subsequently discovered — and told him about

— after she had clarified the matter with an expert. Not surprisingly, he had lost much of his authority in her eyes.

One day he heard that there was a problem about using certain salt shakers on Shabbos. He came home and mentioned this to his wife. She responded with skepticism since in her parents' home they knew of no such restriction. He demanded that she nevertheless refrain from using the salt shaker no matter what they did in her parents' home. "In my home," he declared, "I will not be satisfied with your parents' standards of Shabbos observance!"

That Shabbos he noticed her using the salt shaker. Furious, he grabbed it, flung it from her hand, and accused her of lacking even a minimum amount of religious commitment. All of this was done in the presence of guests. Naturally, it precipitated a major crisis in the marriage.

Ostensibly, the argument was over Halacha, but of course this was not the true issue. He was retaliating for the blows to his self-esteem which he had suffered when he had not known the correct Halacha, and he was now desperately trying to re-establish himself as the house Halachic authority. Furthermore, he had been frequently annoyed in the past because she showed more respect to her parents than to him. This made him very resentful over her reference to how her parents acted in their home.

She, on the other hand, resisted his request not to use the salt shaker because she sensed, correctly, that his request was motivated by self-interest rather than concern for Halacha. She felt he was using the newly introduced law to demean her parents as ignoramuses, lax in their Shabbos observance. Even more important, she felt he was trying to put her down as well, since, after all, she had grown up in their home.

Thus, what was actually at stake in the argument was a battle over prestige — plus retaliation for past offenses to each other's honor. Until this fact was recognized it was impossible to end the argument. Once it was recognized, it was possible to bring the row under control.

It is especially important to recognize anger which stems from past grievances. As discussed earlier, people tend to retaliate not only for the present offense, but for similar offenses in the past.

This situation can be avoided. One should never let grievances pile up. Problems should be discussed as soon as feasible after they arise. Of course, they should not be discussed where there is a chance that this will reawaken the anger. The discussions should be held calmly, and the air cleared with understanding and mutual trust.

Complaints which husband and wife have against one another should not be permitted to fester. It is a good idea never to go to sleep without settling a grievance. At the very least, one should make every effort (as the Sages say[8]) to be at perfect peace with his wife by the time Shabbos arrives.

Grievances should be considered on their own merits. Taken on their own, grievances will often have very little substance. (Is it *really* that tragic if a wife is a little late or if she forgets to prepare a meal on time?) Avoid the inclination to administer collective punishment for past misdeeds whenever a present misdeed is perpetrated. Decide whether the current episode is enough reason to get angry. The worst time to collect outstanding debts is while upset.

Exploded Fantasies

The grievances which anger the husband could be of his own making. When a man enters a marriage with unrealistic expectations about marriage, he will blame his wife for the gap between reality and his fantasy. Why didn't she create the instant bliss which every wife is supposed to create? Why does she have faults? Why are there financial and other problems? Why is he not as successful in his studies and other activities as he had hoped to be? All these grievances can be resolved by an awareness of the realities of marriage, as discussed in Chapter Three. A regular review of that chapter will put these grievances into their proper perspective.

Shifting the Blame

We protect our pride by blaming others for our faults. It is one of the human being's most ingrained reactions. The first person to do so was the very first person, Adam, who reacted to God's question about whether he ate from the Tree of Knowledge in this manner: "The woman You gave me, she gave me from the tree and I ate."[9] There is a very compelling logic to this technique: it helps us maintain an untarnished self-image of ourselves.

Through improper education, many parents inculcate this approach to problems in their children. If a toddler falls he is instructed to spank the "naughty, naughty ground" which hurt him, instead of being instructed how to be more careful next time. If repeated enough times, this can form an attitude which will be carried through life.

Blaming others can be carried to ridiculous extremes. We fail a test. Our reaction is likely to be: "I hate myself for this; I am always making these stupid mistakes." Of course the last person we hate is ourselves. But somehow by giving the stupidity within ourselves (the "I" which makes the mistakes) the status of an autonomous personality, we (the "I" which is doing the blaming) are able to shift the blame and to feel that we are exonerated from guilt.

By refusing to accept responsibility for our short-comings and faults, we do ourselves damage: we will never be prompted to improve ourselves or to avoid re-currences of the failure. Nevertheless, most people are not prepared to take personal responsibility for their lives, and are constantly blaming others.

The most convenient person to blame is one's wife. She is, of course, the most readily available. In addition, the fantasy persists, whether consciously or uncon-sciously, that if she would have been the perfect person he imagined her to be, no problems would have arisen. For these reasons, she becomes a scapegoat.

Thus, if a husband has not been successful in study or in work, she is to blame — since if she would have made him happier, he would have been able to concentrate better. If they do not have enough money, it is her fault for not shopping wisely, for wasting money on frivolous expenditures, for not managing on less, or even for not having wealthy parents. Many husbands attribute a lifetime of problems to their wives.

It is especially important to resist the urge to shift the blame to others when one has just faced a setback. At times like this, a husband should make an extra effort to be kind, courteous, and pleasant to his wife to avoid making her the scapegoat.

Frumkeit/*Piety*

For someone who considers Torah and mitzvos to be of paramount importance, being considered a pious Jew is the ultimate prestige. But it is more difficult to protect oneself from anger when these form the basis of a clash since (as we have noted in our study of the story of Hillel) we have less moral drive to resist the urge for anger when we feel self-righteous.

Someone, for instance, may decide to spend several days, if necessary, to find a perfect *esrog* for Sukkos. Since the *esrog* has become his status emblem, he will treat anyone who interferes with his efforts as inconsiderate of his honor. Thus, if his wife asks him to interrupt his search to help her with preparations for the festival, he may treat this as he would any other affront: with anger. The problem is compounded by the fact that he will feel so self-righteous about his *esrog* that he will find it difficult to restrain himself.

Similarly, a man who is annoyed by his wife's requests that he help her might be able to control his reactions under ordinary circumstances. But if she interrupts him while he is studying Torah, or on his way to do so, he will find himself becoming very annoyed. He feels that he has a right to be angry because what he is doing at that time is so much more important than whatever she wants him to do.

The noblest act (ironically, even an attempt at self-training in humility) can sometimes be a source of pridefulness. One should therefore be doubly careful when occupied with a *beyn odom lamakom* (between man and God) mitzvah to make sure that one's intentions are pure.

NOTES TO CHAPTER EIGHT

1. Vilna Gaon, *Beyur al kama agados*, section beginning "בין גלא".
2. *Bava Kama 92b.*
3. Vilna Gaon, *Beyurey HaGra al agados*, Bava Kama, ib.
4. *Mishna Berurah 583, 5.*
5. *Midrash Tanchuma Bereyshis 8.*
6. *Taanis 20b.*
7. *Sefer HaChinuch 582.*
8. *Tikkuney Zohar 21*, quoted in various works.
9. *Bereyshis 3:12.*

9

CONTROLLING ANGER

Having discussed the anger stimuli and their specific responses in the previous chapter, we turn now to some considerations regarding the control of anger.

In brief, since anger is a product of injured pride, it can be controlled only to the extent that we:

> A) reduce the inflated ego which causes us to feel affronted;
> B) analyze if we have imagined or exaggerated the affront (usually the case);
> C) overcome our urge to react to the affront with anger.

Reducing Gaavah

A truly humble person will almost never become angry because, as we have previously noted, he lacks the inflated pride which, when threatened, triggers the anger response. True humility, *anavah*, is the most exalted character attribute to which a Jew can aspire, toward which he should be striving throughout his lifetime. Although very few people ever reach perfect *anavah*, even partial attainments in this area are valuable — and vital.

Contrary to popular opinion, humility is not stupidity. It does not involve closing one's eyes to one's accomplishments or to one's value to the community. Moshe Rabeynu was called the humblest of all men, even though God had told him to write in the Torah that no prophet like himself would ever arise in Israel.[1] Awareness of his exalted level of prophecy did not subvert his humility.

Humility is the ability to recognize one's true worth before his Creator's infinite greatness. With this recognition, a person will not succumb to pride regardless of his advantages over someone else, even if these include the gift of prophecy. Would a freshman physics student attempt to flaunt his wisdom before an Einstein? Even more so, would someone who had just learned how to read Hebrew strut and boast of his wisdom before a world-famous Torah giant? Similarly, when one succeeds in seeing himself as he truly is — an insignificant mortal vis-a-vis the omnipotent and omniscient Master of the Universe, he recognizes the absurdity of defending his microscopic ego.

Although humility requires little more than seeing things as they really are, man's pride makes the perception extremely hard to come by. Pride is really a form of insanity, but it is an insanity universally accepted, and of which one is not easily rid. Many years of searching, training, and prayer must therefore be invested in order to reach any appreciable level of anavah.

The first step towards acquiring this attribute can be taken by responding to ego-threatening situations as if one were truly humble. The famous maxim of the author of the

Messilas Yeshorim has it that external actions evoke internal responses.[2] Therefore, consistently acting *like* an *anav* will ultimately awaken inner feelings of true humility.

Nothing is as effective in awakening these feelings as responding to an anger-provoking situation in the way an *anav* would respond, i.e., with self-control. Every time one does this he has moved that much closer towards acquiring *anavah*. Not only this, but every time one controls his anger he makes it easier for himself to avoid anger the next time.

How an *anav* behaves in the face of an anger-threatening situation can be discerned from the story of the man who tried to anger Hillel.[2a] Hillel treated the man with respect: he sat down next to him (as if to tell him that he need not feel rushed); he spoke calmly to him; he praised his questions; and he displayed a willingness to listen to him. Employing any of these methods reduces the pressure within us to become angry since they are external acts of humility: they both arouse our sense of respect for other people and diminish our own need to demonstrate our superiority.

A valuable weapon in the fight against pride is a sense of humor. The Sages say that all forms of derision *(leytzanus)* are forbidden except for the derision of idolatry.[3] Anger, which the Sages characterize as the worship of the idol within ourselves (self-worship),[4] is exactly what a sense of humor was created for. A self-directed joke often helps to see things in their true proportions and remove the ego pressures which causes anger.

I once heard a wife call her husband a "stupid idiot" in the presence of many guests. Shocked silence followed. But the husband removed the tension by pulling himself up to full height in mock anger and saying: "I resent that. I have been an idiot all my life, but this is the first time someone has implied that I was a stupid one to boot." The joke made everyone laugh. It also made everyone forget — and the wife to feel sorry for — her nasty remark. Most important, through his humor the husband deflated his own ego and sidetracked his anger.

Defusing the Threat

We can neutralize the cause of anger by viewing whatever we believe has threatened our pride in its proper perspective.

Most of the things which agitate us are meaningless trivialities: Someone forgot our birthday; someone forgot to invite us to their wedding; someone neglected to give us an honor in *shul* — all of these are pitifully inconsequential. Does the birthday or wedding really mean so much to us? And, who remembers who was called to the Torah reading after a day or two? In fact, most pretexts for anger could be neutralized if we would only think to ourselves: "Will this bother me in two weeks or in two years?"

Furthermore, what we consider to be a malevolent offense often turns out to be entirely unintentional. If someone telephones for a taxi and the taxi does not appear, he will probably get angry at the dispatcher for his "nerve" in keeping him waiting. A little thought, however, will make it clear that the dispatcher was not in the least

interested in hurting his customer. He neglected to send
out the taxi due to considerations much closer to his heart:
he had a better-paying customer; he had no taxis to send;
or he simply forgot. But the last thing on the dispatcher's
mind was offending a passenger whom he barely knows
and whose future patronage he desires.

The same is true for most matters which we consider
insults: they are usually imagined and/or exaggerated.

But even if the offense is not imagined, is it possible to
believe that it is worth destroying the most precious gift of
marriage because of it? Yet this is what anger does.
Looked at in this perspective, there is *nothing* important
enough to get angry over.

False Interpretations

In the previous chapter, which dealt with the various
stimuli to anger, we discussed the problem of reading over-
tones into innocent acts and of "collecting debts" for past
grievances whenever there is a slight provocation which
somehow resembles the earlier deed. Grievances, we
noted, should be treated on their own merits, and the habit
of collective punishment should be avoided. In this
chapter, which deals with controlling anger, we discuss a
very important method of counteracting angry responses
to innocent acts.

One of the mitzvos of the Torah is that of giving
someone the benefit of the doubt: "Judge your neighbor
fairly."[5] This mitzvah, commonly referred to as *limud
lekaf zechus*, requires us to judge a person favorably in a

situation where his action might be interpreted as either
well- or ill-intended.

How far our obligation goes in this area is illustrated
by the following story from the Talmud.[6]

> A man went down from the Upper Galilee to hire himself
> out to a certain householder in the South for three years.
> Erev Yom Kippur (at the end of his term of service) he
> said to his employer: "Give me my wages and I will go
> and feed my wife and children."
>
> "I have no money," he replied.
>
> "Then give me produce," the worker beseeched.
>
> Answered the householder, "I have none."
>
> "Give me land," the worker asked desperately.
>
> "I have none."
>
> "Give me cattle."
>
> "I have none."
>
> "Give me pillows and blankets."
>
> "I have none."
>
> The hired hand dejectedly packed his belongings on his
> back and returned home.
>
> After the holiday, the householder piled three
> donkeyloads, one of food, one of drink and one of
> delicacies as the worker's wages and travelled to the
> house of the worker. They ate and drank together and
> afterward he gave him his wages.
>
> "Tell me," the householder asked of the worker. "When
> you demanded, 'Give me my wages' and I answered, 'I
> have none,' what did you suspect me of?"
>
> "I thought perhaps you had the opportunity to buy goods
> cheaply, and you bought them with the money you owed
> me."

"And when you asked, 'Give me cattle' and I said, 'I have no cattle,' what did you then suspect me of?"

"I thought that perhaps they were hired out to someone else."

"And when you begged me, 'Give me land,' and I said, 'I have no land,' what did you think then?"

"I thought perhaps it had been leased out to someone."

And when I told you, 'I have no produce,' what did you believe was the truth?"

"I thought perhaps you had not yet tithed them."

"And when I said: 'I have no pillows and blankets,' what did you suspect?"

"I thought perhaps you had sanctified them all to the Temple."

The householder turned towards his worker with great emotion and said: "I swear to you that this is what actually happened: I had made a vow of abstinence not to have benefit from any of my property because of my son, Horkynos, who did not want to study Torah. But when I came to my colleagues in the academy of the South, they absolved me of all my vows. As for you, just as you have given me the benefit of the doubt, may God judge you the same way!"

To reinforce this idea, and to demonstrate that we are sometimes even obligated to bend over backward to justify a righteous man, the Talmud follows this story with another:

The Rabbis taught: A very pious man, accompanied by his students, once redeemed a young Jewish girl from captivity by Gentiles. On their way home, when they lodged, he made sure that the girl slept at the foot of his bed. The next morning, before teaching his students

Torah, he immersed himself in a *mikveh* [in the manner of someone who has had an emission of seed].

The rabbi thought that perhaps his students suspected him of having committed an immoral act during the night. He asked them: "When I ordered her to sleep at my foot-rest why did you think I did this?"

"We thought that this was perhaps because one of us was not trustworthy in our master's eyes."

"And when I went down to immerse myself, what did you suspect?"

"We thought that our master had a nocturnal emission which is usual after the exhaustion of travelling."

"I swear to you that this was exactly what happened. As for you, just as you have given me the benefit of the doubt, so may God judge you the same way."

There are many reasons for this mitzvah to judge a neighbor fairly. First, as the above passage explains, God treats us the way we treat our fellow man. If we judge others with generosity of spirit, God judges us in like manner, *midah kenegged midah* (measure for measure). Thus, giving another person the benefit of the doubt increases God's mercy toward us.

Second, if we learn to look benevolently at the world, our own religious level rises. Because no one wants to be the first person to do evil, if we give our neighbor the benefit of the doubt and assume that he did no wrong, it will then be that much more difficult for us to do evil ourselves.[7]

Finally, the most powerful reason for this mitzvah is that nothing prevents a quarrel more effectively than giving the other person the benefit of the doubt. If we can assume that our friend has done us no harm, or that he had no malicious intention even if he did inadvertently do us harm, we will have no reason to become angry with him.

The mitzvah of *limud lekaf zechus* is spelled out by Rabbeynu Yonah in his *Shaarey Teshuvah*[8]:

> If you see someone saying something or performing an act and the words or act can be judged to have either a good or evil intention, then if the person in question is a God-fearing person, you are obligated to give him the benefit of the doubt in a manner [by which you would consider this to be] the truth. This is even if the matter is closer to, and is more probably of, an evil nature.

> If the person is one of the average people who are careful at times not to sin but who sometimes stumble into a transgression, you are obligated to take one side of the doubt and give him the benefit of the doubt....

> If the matter tends to the side of evil and the person is one whose acts are generally evil, or you have ascertained that there is no fear of God in his heart, you may decide all his actions and words by assuming that he acted with an evil intention."

How many times is quarreling triggered by a husband's mistaken assumption that his wife has intentionally harmed or insulted him? If his first reaction would be to recall his Torah obligation to give her the benefit of the doubt, the fight would never have started.

Discussion of the Offense

> Whoever hates a single Jew in his heart violates a negative commandment.... When a person commits evil against his friend, [the victim] should neither hate him nor

refrain from telling him [his feelings]...but he is obligated
to inform him [of the grudge he bears against him] and to
say to him, "Why did you do such and such to me; why
have you wronged me in that particular matter?" — as it
is written, "הוכח תוכיח את עמיתך" — "You must rebuke
your friend."[9]

Rambam Deyos 6:6

It is therefore clearly forbidden to harbor unspoken
complaints; one must bring any perceived offense to the
other person's attention.

Nine times out of ten this will forestall an argument.
The person to whom the complaint is revealed will
probably have some explanation for his wrongdoing. If he
does not, he will at least have the opportunity to apologize.
The cause of any anger will thereby be removed.

Overcoming the Urge

If none of these approaches quells one's urge to anger,
the following suggestions should prove helpful.

Keep silent. It is difficult to quarrel with one's mouth
closed. A Chassidic Rebbe used to dispense "holy water"
guaranteed to eliminate all domestic fights. Whenever a
husband or wife had an urge to argue, he or she was told to
hold some of this water in his or her mouth without
swallowing it for as long as he or she could. This "holy
water" was, not surprisingly, extremely effective in
stopping the squabble.

One important point should be noted: while it is
"difficult" to argue with one's mouth closed, it is not
impossible. For even without speaking one can quarrel by

slamming a door, pounding on a table, grimacing, or making threatening motions. All of these can ignite a domestic battle, and a gallant effort should be made to avoid this silent arguing as well. Nevertheless, none of these is as dangerous as actual words spoken in anger. Therefore, one's major efforts should be directed towards maintaining verbal silence at all costs, even if body language is not under control.

A corollary of the technique of silence, often very effective, is the delaying action. Wait to get angry for, say, fifteen minutes (or even better, a full day). In the meantime get busy doing something else, preferably in another room (without slamming the door when leaving). Almost invariably you will have a different perspective on the issue after the delay, and very rarely will you actually become angry.

If you must give voice to your anger, do it in solitude. Go into a room where no one can hear you and shout. Preferably, do this in front of a mirror. Listening and watching yourself fulminate and exaggerate will help defuse your anger. No one respects an angry man, least of all yourself. Quite possibly you might even start laughing at yourself — which, incidentally, will often be the reaction of anyone who witnesses you when you are angry.

The procedures used by a certain department store to handle telephone complaints are instructive. The individual whose job it was to handle the complaints was trained to ask her caller if he "would kindly repeat" what he said because she "did not get it straight" the first time. The caller would, of course, repeat his complaint — but would usually tone down his anger appreciably the second time around. The next step was to transfer his call to another operator who would also ask him to repeat his complaint — for a third time. By this time the caller had lost most of his heat, and the apology offered by the telephone operator was generally accepted.

The principles behind this tactic are: a) delay weakens anger; b) hearing oneself getting angry makes one feel a little silly. Most people would prefer to stop arguing rather than relive the experience of sounding like a fool. These same methods can be employed by anyone who feels that anger is about to overcome him.

Even more effective than these ploys, if one can manage clear thinking, is the recollection of one's obligations as a Jew. The Torah forbids anger, except in rare circumstances. Anger also brings about other innumerable violations of the Torah. Chief among these is the prohibition against causing any Jew anguish, "לא תונו "איש את עמיתו — "You shall not [verbally] oppress your friend."[10] But there are many more, as listed in Chapter Four.

Whenever a Jew who is committed to Torah has an urge to get angry, he should try to imagine that he has before him a forbidden dish of meat and milk mixed together. Would he consider eating this mixture? The transgression of becoming angry is at least, if not more, serious. Why should one be willing to violate one transgression and not the other?

Another way of arousing one's religious sensibilities is to picture oneself on Erev Yom Kippur contritely begging

his wife's forgiveness for all the times he has offended her.
Wouldn't it make sense to prevent this?

We should note God's own way of loving man even at
the very moment when man is deserving of punishment.
The verse says, "ברגז רחם תזכור" — "At a time of anger He
reminds himself of His mercy (love)."[11] At the moment of
anger at his wife, a husband should, in imitation of God's
ways, remind himself of his love for her. He should recall
the close moments they have had together; recall their
wedding day; think of all the wonderful things she has
done for him, of all she has sacrificed for his comfort and
benefit; realize that she is actually part of him, and that
fighting with her is the equivalent of fighting with himself.

If anger still cannot be contained, one should at the
very least follow Hillel's example: speak in a calm voice.
This will reduce the level of anger no matter how one feels
inside. "מענה רך ישיב חמה" — "A calm voice removes
anger," says the wisest of all men.[12]

How to Quarrel

If you must quarrel, there are some ground rules by
which you should abide.

Firstly, keep it private. Never argue in public, and
even in your own home, close the windows and doors: the
neighbors do not have to be entertained. Spare yourself —
and your wife — the embarrassment of public knowledge
of your anger.

Never mention or hint at divorce. When you start talking about divorce, you are cutting into your wife and are

seriously undermining the foundations of your marriage. The quarrel will eventually be forgotten, but if you mention divorce the wounds may continue to fester.

Remember that you will have to answer for whatever you say. Keep the fight as clean as possible. Do not use expressions or epithets that may haunt you later.

Try to avoid generalizations. Make it a point *never* to use the word "always" (e.g., "You are *always* doing this to me"). You will be surprised how much hurt and anger can be avoided by avoiding this single word.

Stick to the issues. Don't use an argument as an excuse for dragging in long-forgotten grievances.

Don't bring up relatives. If you are angry with your wife this is not the time to insert a gratuitous insult about her parents.

Avoid psychological analysis. Showing that your wife's problems are incurable or hereditary makes absolutely no difference. You want a happy marriage — not to prove that she is psychologically inferior to you.

Be ready to compromise. You do not always have to have your way. If she is ready to give in a little, show that you are willing to do so as well.

Finally, make up as soon as possible after the fight. Be prepared to apologize even if you are not at fault, and certainly if you were. When you apologize, make sure you do not suffice with the simple words, "I am sorry." These words are cheap and often do not remove the source of the quarrel. It is important to elaborate on why you are sorry, to explain why you think you were wrong. Most important of all, do not sulk while you apologize. Sulking is a childish way of evoking another person's pity. It does nothing to end the argument. The open admission of your error will only increase your wife's respect for you and will make another fight less likely.

A good piece of advice from the Chafetz Chayim about arguments over money (quite a common cause) should be noted: Most of these quarrels are over petty amounts. Yet, people fight over these sums because they feel that if they yield once, there will be no end to the amount of money they will ultimately have to spend. The truth is that an honest reckoning would show that the most one stands to lose — even if he gives in each time to these petty arguments — is a relatively small amount, perhaps, fifty dollars a year. Anger and bickering are so spiritually devastating that it is obviously not worth it. It would therefore be a good idea to set aside a certain amount of money as a fund from which to "draw" whenever the urge arises to argue over money. In other words, whenever this temptation arises, one should yield to the other person and deduct the disputed amount from his fund. If one has an argument with, say, a storekeeper over whether the latter has overcharged him by some amount, and he feels himself becoming angry, let him yield to the storekeeper and "use" the money from this fund to cover his expenses. The total amount lost yearly will certainly be less than the amount he spends on other mitzvos, say *matzos* or *sukkah*. Spending money to avoid falling into the evil of quarrelling is certainly at least as important as spending money for any other Torah obligation.[13]

This method can be successfully used to avert arguments with a wife over monetary affairs. The mitzvah of *Shalom Bayis* (marital peace) is one of the most important in the Torah, and therefore one should be prepared to enter into unnecessary expenditures if this will calm the air.

The Tefillin *and the* Esrog

A man had no money to buy an *esrog* for Sukkos. His wife had an exceptional pair of *tefillin* which she had inherited from her father and had given him in her dowry. Since the husband owned another pair of *tefillin* he decided to sell those *tefillin* to buy himself an *esrog* with the proceeds.

At the end of the day, he returned home beaming with joy, with an excellent and expensive *esrog* in his hands. His wife couldn't believe her eyes. "Where on earth did you get money to buy such a beautiful *esrog?*" she asked.

"I sold your father's *tefillin* — they were not being used anyway."

The wife exploded in anger. "You fool! You dared sell my father's *tefillin?*" She lunged at her husband and knocked the *esrog* out of his hands. It fell to the ground and a piece broke off, making it *possul* (unfit for use) — and worthless. The man calmly bent over, picked up the *esrog*, held it in his hand to appraise the damage — but didn't say a word. And then, after a few moments, he suddenly began singing and dancing. His wife looked at him in amazement. "Are you out of your mind?" she asked. "Not at all," he said, obviously very happy. "I lost my precious *tefillin*; I lost my perfect *esrog*. But I was able to control myself and I did not lose my *Shalom Bayis*. Could anything be more of a reason for joy?"

NOTES TO CHAPTER NINE

1. *Devorim 34:10.*
2. R. Moshe Chayim Luzzato, *Messilas Yesharim*, Chapter 7.
2a. *Shabbos 80*. See Chapter Seven where this is treated at length.
3. *Megillah 25b.*
4. *Shabbos 105b.*
5. *Vayikra 19:16.*
6. *Shabbos 127b*. See *Maharatz Chayes, ad loc.* that one Gaon writes that the worker in this story was the Sage, Rabbi Akiva.
7. R. Yehoshua Leyb Diskin, *Teshuvos Maharil*, end of Part One.
8. Rabbeynu Yonah, *Shaarey Teshuvah*, Sec. 3:218.
9. *Vayikra 19:17.*
10. *Vayikra 25:17.*
11. *Havakuk 3:2.*
12. *Mishley 15:1.*
13. Chafetz Chayim (R. Yisroel Meir HaKohen), *Shemiras HaLashon*, end of Sec. 1.

10

THE FUTILITY OF ANGER

Besides the Torah prohibition, the most compelling reason for eschewing anger is its futility. As the Sages say, "רגזן אין לו אלא רגזנותיה" — "An angry man is left with nothing but his anger."[1] Since nothing else is ever gained, he is left with anger alone.

By getting angry in response to an affront, an individual believes that he will accomplish one or both of the following goals:

> A) *he will restore his lost prestige;*
> B) *he will prevent a repetition of the affront.*

But neither goal is likely to be achieved.[2]

Let us first consider the fallacy of the first goal: why prestige — or respect — cannot be regained through anger.

How Respect Is Earned

The Sages tell us:

כל המחזר על הגדולה גדולה בורחת ממנו,
וכל הבורח מן הגדולה גדולה מחזרת אחריו

> Whoever pursues importance finds that importance
> escapes him;
> whoever runs from importance finds that importance
> pursues him.[3]

In other words, respect cannot be gained by pursuing it directly. This requires some explanation.

We naturally feel that human beings are more worthy of respect than animals. It follows that the more "human" a person is (i.e., the less animal-like) the more he deserves our respect. We never respect someone on account of attributes he shares with animals, e.g., he is someone who can eat a whole lamb or sleep uninterruptedly for twenty-four hours. But we do respect someone who is gifted with a noble character, wisdom or artistic talent — all specifically human qualities.

This is why selfless individuals are universally admired. These are people so committed to humanistic ideals that they pursue them at great cost to themselves, regardless of what others think of them. No animal ever does anything except in response to its instinctual drives. Because selfless people have risen above their animal instincts, they are recognized by us as truly accomplished human beings. This is what elicits our respect for them.

In the same vein is the Sages' comment that "whoever studies Torah in private, will have his glory proclaimed by the Torah in public."[4] For whoever studies Torah in private — i.e., not for the sake of the glory which this will bring him, but because he is devoted to the pursuit of truth — will be recognized as a great human being. This means that his selfless devotion to spiritual matters will permit everyone to clearly see that he is a person who has risen above the animal instincts within him. As a result, he will have earned true glory. As the Sages put it, the Torah which he pursues so selflessly will then proclaim his glory in public.

On the other hand, we cannot respect someone who lives for himself and his own personal advancement. We despise people who are motivated by animalistic self-interest.

This, then, is the theory behind the Sages' paradox that glory runs away from one who seeks it, yet pursues one who runs from it. The very act of seeking after glory demeans its seeker in the eyes of observers. By demonstrating his lust for honor, by displaying his hungry pursuit of self-interest, he reveals his crass, animal nature — and thereby loses our respect.

Accordingly, one who employs anger cannot hope to restore his lost prestige. Fundamentally, anger is an expression of glory-seeking; as such, it condemns its user to disgrace.

Will Anger Stop an Argument?

What about goal (B) of the individual who succumbs to anger: preventing repetitions of the affront? If we think about it, we see that here, too, anger is an exercise in futility.

How do you expect your insults to prevent further affronts to your prestige? The natural reaction to an attack is a counterattack. This is exactly how *you* are reacting to the affront which you have just experienced. It stands to reason that your friend will react in the same way. Thus, as a result of your anger, the affronts will increase in their intensity. Even if the original offense which triggered your anger was unintentional, the subsequent insults will be clearly premeditated.

Rather than ending the argument, anger will only fuel it. If the argument began on one issue it will spread to many more. As the Sages say:

האי תיגרא דמיא לבידקא דמיא כיון דרווח רווח
An argument is like an overflowing stream;
the more it flows, the wider it spreads.[5]

Even if only two people were involved to begin with, there is an ever-present potential that before long your friends and relatives will begin to join in. Other faults which you have, or have had, will be dragged out into the open. Rather than stopping abuse, the path of anger will only add insult to insult.

Anger will only silence your antagonist if you can communicate that you intend to resort to actual violence — provided you are stronger than he is. But even this will only temporarily end the argument. Obviously, as soon as he is out of your reach he will abuse you even more, and — if he is able to do so — will be planning to retaliate. And your lost prestige will certainly not be restored by advertising that you are a violent man.

This process has been summed up perfectly by the Vilna Gaon: Attempting to stop an argument by arguing is the same as trying to wash one's face in one's filth: the more one washes, the more he sullies himself.[6]

Why an Angry Man Is a Fool

Clearly, as the Sages say, an angry man is left with nothing but his anger.[7] Not only has he failed to accomplish his aims, but he has worsened his position.

This explains why the wisest of men calls an angry man a fool.[8] An angry man expends considerable energy, raises his blood pressure, unplugs his mind — all of this for something which is not only futile but is counter-productive. Only a fool would do such a thing.

The Effect of Anger on a Marriage

If all of this is true of a quarrel with an outsider, how much more so of a quarrel with one's wife.

The Sages say, ‏"האי מאן דמיהר אפילו אאינשי ביתיה לא‎ ‏מיקבל‎" — "A prideful man is not even acceptable to his own wife."[9] A woman wants to become close to a husband who is concerned with her. A prideful man demonstrates that his ego is his main concern. A wife cannot be blamed if she suspects that she is not his main concern. It is normal, therefore, that anger — which is an expression of pridefulness — will cause a wife to feel distant from her husband.

Few things ruin the fabric of a marriage relationship more than anger. For a marriage to be successful there has to be, as we have already noted, a feeling of mutual concern and love. The only emotion which anger engenders is fear. Fear and love (except in one's relationship to God) are mutually exclusive emotions, and it is therefore impossible to love a menacing and angry husband.

The Proper Response to an Affront

If anger is not the correct response, what is the best way to react to an affront? How can one realize the aims which anger necessarily fails to achieve: regaining respect and stopping future abuse? There is only one way: the control of anger.

Containing anger gains respect because self-control is one of those elevated human qualities of character which, as we have noted, is the key to eliciting respect. In addition, when a witting offender sees that his victim is able to control his temper (something the offender was not able to do), he will feel ashamed of himself, ashamed enough to refrain from further attacks. Finally, the quarrel will stop for a simple reason: it takes two to argue. When the offender sees that his victim does not respond, he will stop his abuse. Control of anger is therefore the best way — the proven way — to put an end to arguments.

NOTES TO CHAPTER TEN

1. *Kiddushin 41a.*
2. The following is based on the Vilna Gaon to *Mishley 30:32.*
3. *Eyruvin 13b.*
4. *Mo'ed Katan 16b.*
5. *Sanhedrin 7a.*
6. Vilna Gaon, *Commentary to Mishley, ib.*
7. *Kiddushin ib.*
8. *Koheles 7:9.*
9. *Sotah 47b.*

11

LOVE AND ITS CATALYSTS

According to the Vilna Gaon, marriage has not arrived at its ultimate purpose until husband and wife create an emotional bond between them strong enough to make them feel that they are two parts of a single organism.[1]

The Sages teach us that man and woman were originally created as one body, but that subsequently God sundered them into male and female beings.[2] God's original plan was that they end up as two separate entities. Why, then, did He create them at first as one unit? Wouldn't it have been much simpler to have created them from the outset — in accordance with His plan — as two separate entities?

The Vilna Gaon explains this as follows:

> ...God created them as one unit in order that there exist a love and brotherhood between them closer than that between siblings or other relatives; that they literally [sense themselves to] be parts of one body.[3]

In other words, although God's original plan was for man and woman to exist as two entities — as, indeed, He ultimately caused them to be — He nevertheless created them first as part of one organism in order to implant within them the permanent sensation of having once belonged to one body. With this sensation in their subconscious, even after having been sundered apart, they would find it easier to create between them a love deeper than any other love in existence.

These intimate emotional bonds between man and wife are apparently so vital for the human condition that God "went to the trouble" of adding another step to man's creation to ensure that they would develop. Why are they so important?

Let us recall that the purpose of marriage is to make it possible for man to redirect his natural inclination for self-worship toward concern for others.[4] Man was created to worship God, but he can only do this if he first learns to stop worshipping himself. In light of this, the potential for close emotional bonds between husband and wife is vital for human existence because it enables man to reach the aims of his creation. In other words, love in marriage is a necessary aspect of human life because it is the major means by which one human being learns to concern himself with another. Creating the capacity for that love is as important as the creation of man himself, important enough for God to have added another step in the process of Creation.

Fostering Love

How does one go about creating this relationship? Fortunately, the Vilna Gaon offers guidance on this matter, as well. There are, he says, four basic causes, or catalysts, of love:

A) *We love someone who gives us physical pleasure.*

B) *We love someone who assists us in accomplishing our goals.*

C) *We love someone in whom we recognize noble qualities of character.*

D) *We love someone for no conscious reason other than that we sense that he loves us.* [5]

Creating love in a marriage therefore requires one or more of these catalysts to be operating. It would seem so simple to create love that one wonders why there are so many people in this world who hate one another. The reason for this is that these four catalysts operate only if the following four preconditions are met:

a) that we are able to feel gratitude (necessary for A and B);
b) that we have goals in our lives (necessary for B);
c) that we are not so preoccupied with our own ego that we fail to recognize good qualities in someone else (necessary for C);
d) that we are able to believe that someone else loves us (necessary for D).

Love is rare because these preconditions go against the grain of our natural selfishness. On the other hand, if we would direct our efforts toward meeting these preconditions, love between husband and wife (as well between all human beings) would be much more prevalent.

The following chapter will help us understand what keeps us from meeting the first precondition, a feeling of gratitude.

NOTES TO CHAPTER ELEVEN

1. Vilna Gaon, *Commentary to Mishley 9:10.*
2. *Kesubos 8a; Eyruvin 18a;* this follows the Gaon's interpretation of these passages of the Talmud. .
3. Same as Note 1.
4. See Chapter Two.
5. Vilna Gaon, *Commentary* to *Shir HaShirim 5:2,* based on his interpretation of "אחותי רעיתי יונתי תמתי". *"Achosi"* ("my sister") refers to love based on utilitarian benefit, generally the reason for family love. *"Ra'ayasi"* ("my mate") refers to love stemming from pleasure. *"Yonasi"* ("my dove") refers to reciprocated love not based on reason. *"Tamasi"* ("my perfect one") refers to love based on recognition of noble qualities. (There is a misprint in the text of the Commentary, as is evident from the *Likkutim, ad loc., s.v. kad.*)

12

GRATITUDE

I was once approached by a husband who complained that his wife was extremely negligent in caring for their home. Instead of washing the dishes and straightening up the kitchen after supper, she would sink into a sofa for the rest of the evening and read a book.

When I questioned the wife about this, she readily admitted that this was all true. She added that she worked twelve hours a day on two jobs to support her husband's study in a *kollel*, and was pregnant besides. By the time she had finished eating dinner, she had no strength left to do anything but relax and read a book.

Obviously, the husband was guilty of gross ingratitude. Although he was the beneficiary of extraordinary sacrifices by his wife, not only did he not feel in the least beholden to her, but he was upset with her for not-doing more for him.

This story illustrates a common fault among men: an inability to properly appreciate the good which their wives do for them.

This inability is remarkable. In light of the enormous amount of physical, emotional, and practical benefits which most men receive from their wives, one might expect that it should not be a difficult task to be thankful to them. Unfortunately, the opposite is true.

This is due, first of all, to the basic human inclination toward refusing to recognize favors received from others. This turns out to be all the more true with regard to favors a wife does for her husband.

What Causes Ingratitude?

Human ingratitude is an evil which stems from Adam. Man's first sin — the source of all evil in him — originated from a refusal to recognize the good with which God had blessed him.[1] If he would not have taken for granted the infinite good which God had bestowed upon him, he never would have eaten from the forbidden Tree of Knowledge. A sense of gratitude would have made it impossible for him to have contravened God's will.

His answer to God when asked if he ate from the Tree underscores this ingratitude: "The woman *whom You gave me* fed me from the tree and I ate."[2] Adam was, in effect, saying: "I didn't ask for her; she was Your idea. If she persuaded me to sin, the sin is Your fault." Although the Torah explicitly tells us that God created woman for man's good (because it was "not good for man to be alone"[3]), Adam failed to recognize this good. This ingratitude is the underlying cause of his sin.

What was true for Adam remains true for all his

descendants: ingratitude is the fundamental source of whatever evil they commit.

Anyone who would pause to recognize that he owes God his very existence would never be able to go through life worshipping himself. Millions of miracles make up man's world: the miracle of nature, the miracle of life, the miracle of sight, of speech, of movement, of marriage, the miracle of being permitted to know God. Man's heart should be full of joy, amazement and thankfulness for the bountiful world with which God has supplied him.

Instead, man considers all of this something which God owes him as his birthright. His pride convinces him that the world exists for his sole use. As Pharaoh said, "The river is mine and I have created myself."[4] Man thus treats whatever is given to him as nothing more than the return of goods to their rightful owner. He owes no thanks for a world which belongs to him before he even takes possession of it.

It is clear, therefore, why gratitude is so rare. The same pride which does not permit man to recognize God's good militates against his recognizing the good bestowed by another human being.

There is an additional impediment to recognizing favors others do for us: it forces us to abandon the fantasy that we are self-sufficient and in charge of our own destiny. It calls upon us to offer thanks to someone else; it obligates us to reciprocate with an equivalent good. Because of this, our natural reaction is to minimize or even to deny the importance of any favor done for us.

If gratitude to anyone is hard to manage, gratitude to a wife is all the more difficult. The favors she confers upon us exceed those of any other person, and therefore the degree of gratitude she deserves is that much more painful to acknowledge and express.

Furthermore, showing gratitude to a wife is more difficult than showing gratitude to a stranger because of the false conception which most husbands have of marriage. As noted above, husbands commonly imagine that it is the natural duty of a wife to bring unending bliss to her husband by satisfying his every whim and desire. Accordingly, it is her duty to supply him with all his needs, and to do anything necessary to advance his ambitions, even to support him financially. It is her duty to see to it that her husband is successful in all his endeavors, whether in his studies, his business, or whatever. It is her duty to do anything anytime to make him happy.

If all this is her natural duty, then she deserves no more thanks for any favor she confers upon him than does a debtor who repays a loan to his creditor: she is merely discharging her obligation.

Of course this betrays gross ignorance of a wife's obligations. She has no responsibility to make her husband happy. If there is any such special obligation it is the husband's to make his wife happy.[5] It is not her duty to ensure that he be successful in his undertakings; this is up to him alone. Furthermore, she has no obligation to contribute to the financial support of the household.

Although a wife is required by rabbinic law to perform

certain household duties, it is the sole duty of her husband to support her. This is clearly stated in the *kesubah* which every husband gives his wife during the wedding ceremony in which he clearly undertakes to "feed, cherish, sustain, and support" her "in the manner of Jewish husbands." Any woman who helps support the family, as is common nowadays, does so beyond the call of Halachic duty. She has every right to stop doing so when she wishes, and to have her husband earn all the income necessary to support her. Such a request would be enforced by any Jewish court. If a woman works out of the goodness of her heart or out of a devotion to her husband's Torah learning, she deserves all the thanks due a philanthropist.

Because gratitude is a precondition to the creation of love in a marriage, one must expend much effort to acquire it. If one will set aside a little time daily — even five minutes — to consider the benefits he has received during the day from his wife, gratitude will eventually become a natural reaction.

How Great Is the Obligation to Be Grateful?

Not only is ingratitude the source of the first sin of man, gratitude is one of the central commandments of the Torah. Among the first ten commandments given to the Jewish people on Mount Sinai is the requirement to honor father and mother.[6] This· mitzvah is an obligation incumbent upon children (regardless of age) to show thankfulness to their parents for having bestowed life upon them and for having reared them.[7]

The Torah is replete with examples of the primary importance of *hakaras-hatov*/gratitude. We are enjoined to treat Egyptians better than other peoples because we were sojourners in their land[8] — even though they enslaved us. Moshe was commanded by God Himself to go and redeem the Jewish people, but he would not do so until he had received permission to leave the house of his father-in-law, Yisro. The reason for this was that he owed Yisro a debt of gratitude: Yisro had opened his house to Moshe when he had escaped to Midyan.[9] Thus, in the event of a conflict between the obligation to show gratitude and the obligation to redeem the Jewish people, gratitude takes precedence.

Moshe would not strike the Nile River to bring the plague of frogs upon the Egyptians because he owed the river a debt of gratitude: it had saved his life when he was an infant.[10] The concept of gratitude applies even to inanimate objects.

Myriad sources in the both the written and Oral Torahs speak of this obligation to show gratitude. No attribute has been more discussed by the great Jewish *mussar* thinkers.

How We Avoid Gratitude

We deny benefits received in two ways: either we conveniently forget to notice or remember them, or we attribute selfish motives to our benefactor.

In the story, cited above, of the unappreciated wife who worked twelve hours a day, there is little doubt that the husband rationalized his lack of gratitude through one or more of the following claims (none of which were true): "It is her duty to support Torah. Besides, it is a woman's nature to be kind to her husband; one need not be appreciative to someone who is forced to act this way. In addition, she is not working for my welfare; she does it for her own good since she enjoys getting out of the house. Also, she wants to pride herself as a successful wife. Furthermore, she wants to please me so that I will love her more. Also, she has a martyr complex: she works beyond the limits of her strength. Come to think of it, she must be quite neurotic to want to work twelve hours a day! She probably wants to impress others with her goodheartedness and devotion. She really does it all for public consumption."

All these rationalizations are based on the misconception that a benefactor's selfish motivation is an excuse for refusing to show gratitude. But even if a wife rendered all of her favors because she thereby derived personal pleasure, or even if she was driven to perform them out of neurotic compulsions, this would not free a husband from being grateful to her. The Egyptians in whose land we were sojourners permitted us to live there for their selfish interests: at first, because Joseph was so important to the country, and then to enslave and exploit the Jewish people. Still, we are obligated to show our appreciation to them. Consider Yisro's motivation: he opened his home to Moshe because he wanted him to marry one of his daughters.[11] Likewise, the commandment to honor father and mother for giving life to their child is the same: their direct intention may very well not have been to give their offspring life. Furthermore, they had no choice, because of their parental instincts, but to raise and care for their child. Yet this commandment is the paradigm of the obligation to show gratitude.

The *Chayyei Odom,* one of the greatest authorities on Halacha in the past 250 years, makes the point forcefully:

> Let the mouths of the speakers of falsehood be sealed who say that one need not be thankful to a father and mother because they intended their personal pleasure and [a child] was born as a result. Also, once he was born [they argue], God made [human] nature such that the mother and father raise their offspring, just as it is the nature of all domesticated and wild animals and birds to raise their offspring; yet their young do not thank them for this.
>
> May [those who argue thus] ...be made deaf and dumb, as it is written, "May the lips of the speakers of falsehood be made mute." They, themselves, testify upon themselves [by their argument] that they are like animals, that they have no portion in [the reward of] God, [nor] a heart that knows and understands.
>
> Regarding this [sort of reasoning] the Sages have said that whoever fails to acknowledge the good bestowed by his fellow will ultimately not recognize the good bestowed by God.[11a] For, according to their reasoning, they do not have to honor and fear God, blessed be He, either; for since we are His creations, it is only proper that He benefit and have mercy on His creations.
>
> There is no doubt that those who speak this way are heretics in their hearts.[12]

Some Reasons for Feeling Gratitude to a Wife

In the Talmud we are told the story of Rabbi Chiyya and his evil wife, a woman who would literally go out of her way to make her husband's life miserable. Whenever he would ask her to prepare a certain food for him, she would deliberately prepare something else. Despite this, whenever he found an item in the market which he thought she would enjoy, he would wrap it in his kerchief and bring it to her as a gift. Rav could not understand this and pointed out to Rabbi Chiyya, "But she causes you so much anguish!" Rabbi Chiyya explained, "It is enough for me that she raises my children and that she saves me from sin."[13]

The evil which his wife had meted out to him did not permit Rabbi Chiyya to forget the benefits received from her. Furthermore, he felt beholden to her for the good which she did not do directly for his benefit: she did not save him from sin out of the goodness of her heart, nor did she raise his children out of love for him but out of her own love for her offspring, an emotion she could hardly avoid.

Despite these considerations Rabbi Chiyya felt so beholden to her that he expressed his appreciation to her with gifts — and not only by an occasional gift. Whenever he found something in the market which he thought she would enjoy, he would buy it for her. And even though she did not reciprocate his kindness and continued to cook him the wrong food deliberately, he continued his practice, because "it is enough that she raises my children and saves me from sin."

If Rabbi Chiyya felt this obligation to an evil wife, how much more so is one obligated to a wife who showers him with favors.

The debt of gratitude one owes to his wife — aside from Rabbi Chiyya's reasons — is limitless. One owes her a debt of gratitude simply for being there. Imagine the utter desolation of living alone and not having someone to whom to say an occasional word. But she is not there merely to have someone with whom to converse. She is a constant companion, available to share every meaningful experience in life.

A man has no greater benefactor than his wife. Even if there is little *Shalom Bayis* in the home she is busy making her husband's life more comfortable and pleasurable. She shops, launders, straightens up the house, prepares food. How much more so is she a benefactor if there is *Shalom Bayis*: she is the closest friend imaginable, devoted to her husband's well-being more than any friend could ever be. Little occupies her mind as much as thoughts of what she can do for her husband and family. His success is her success; his failure, hers. She is loyal and devoted to him beyond anyone else in the world, without expecting anything in return — except to be appreciated and loved by her husband. When the Sages said that a woman illuminates her husband's eyes and puts him on his feet,[14] they were not in the least exaggerating.

Over and above what she does for her husband, her more hidden and indirect benefits are of even a greater scope. Everything about a household which makes it a home is due to a wife. As Rabbi Yochanan said, he never called his wife "my wife," but "my home."[15] She creates its atmosphere, its ambience, its mood. She ensures that it continues along its appointed path toward sacred joy.

Administering a family requires infinite patience, wisdom, decision making, and emotional strength. During the course of an ordinary day she serves as her children's nurturer, educator, and judge. The present and future of her family lie in her hands. Their physical and emotional stability rest upon the manner in which she cares for them, upon tasks which on the surface often seem simple and elementary. She is sensitive to each of their individual requirements. She constantly decides which food is proper for which child; she is responsive to each of their emotional needs and weaknesses; she is ready to render assistance to help in coping with their private fears and struggles. As their educator it is she who inculcates wholesome values, teaches them about God, acts as their model, and forms their attitudes toward life, toward their Creator, toward others, toward themselves — in addition to helping them with their homework. As their constant supervisor she is always on the alert to decide who deserves punishment, who deserves reward, and how to settle sibling squabbles.

The duties performed by a wife in an ordinary day would do honor to a fully-staffed children's clinic. How much, then, does one owe his wife for years upon years of such devoted endeavors. Honestly considered, one can never fully repay the debt of gratitude due to one's wife. But the least one can do is recognize — and appreciate — how vast and vital is her benefaction.

NOTES TO CHAPTER TWELVE

1. See *Bereyshis Rabba* 19, 19.
2. *Bereyshis 3:12.*
3. *Ib. 2:18.*
4. *Yechezkel 29:3.*
5. *SeMaK 285;* but see *Nishmas Odom* to *Chayyei Odom 147, 1,* that most authorities disagree that there is a special positive commandment beyond the first year. There are, however, many general commandments which apply equally to husband and wife throughout marriage; see Chapter Three.
6. *Shemos 20:12.*
7. Sages quoted in *Chayyei Odom 67:1.*
8. *Devarim 23:8.*
9. *Shemos Rabba 4.*
10. *Shemos 7:19* and *Rashi ad loc.*
11. *Shemos 2:20;* see *Rashi ib.*
11a. *Talmud Yerushalmi Berachos 3.*
12. *Chayyei Odom, Hilchos Kibud Av VaEym, 67, 2.*
13. *Yevamos 63a.*
14. *Ib.*
15. *Shabbos 113a.*

13

COMPLETING THE BONDS

One of the catalysts of love, as we noted earlier,[1] is the feeling that someone has assisted us in accomplishing our objectives. This makes us grateful to him, makes us aware of the importance of that other person's contribution to our success in life, and thereby causes love to grow.

Working together towards a common goal induces love for an additional reason; namely, that it evokes a sense of harmony and trust between the two working partners — which strengthens the emotional bonds between them.

Without goals in life none of this is possible. A married couple must be moving toward some common objective if love is to develop between them.

The Importance of Goals

Goals in a marriage are vital not only because they help foster love, but because they are an indispensable ingredient of life itself. There can be no joy to a life which is purposeless, and married life is no exception.

A marriage whose goal is the marriage itself becomes filled with a sense of emptiness and will wither and die. Marriage is not meant to be a permanent "date." The purpose of the marriage cannot be simply doing fun things together. The sole occupation of a marriage cannot be entertainment, idle conversation, or other trivia. It must be a vehicle for getting somewhere. In a world where few people have goals for their lives, this explains why so many marriages fail.

This does not mean that a couple always has to be doing the same things, going the same places, enjoying the same activities. But there must be some common goals present for marriage to have any direction and for the emotional relationship between husband and wife to grow.

The Sages' use of the term *Shalom Bayis* to describe a happy home corroborates this idea. *Shalom* means peace. Peace in itself can never be said to be a goal of life. Would any nation declare that its ultimate aim is to be merely eternally at peace with other nations? Peace, at the most, is the framework for whatever goals the nation strives to reach. Similarly, marital peace can only create the framework in which a couple can achieve life's goals.

All common goals form the earth in which marriage flourishes. But the more important the goals, the deeper the emotional bonds created by working towards achieving them. A marriage is thus successful in proportion to the meaningfulness of the couple's common activities.

Nothing can be as meaningful or as encompassing as the goal of making one's home a sanctuary for God, a home built on Torah and mitzvos. Accordingly, nothing has a greater capacity for creating love in a marriage than striving to reach these goals. For this reason (contrary to what most people believe) the most nearly complete *Shalom Bayis* reigns in the home of *tzaddikim* (perfectly righteous Jews) committed to building a home for the service of God.

A few years ago, Rabbi Shlomo Zalman Auerbach, one of the leading Torah sages of our times, lost his wife of over fifty years. Before thousands of people who gathered to pay their last respects to her, Rav Shlomo Zalman eulogized her in a moving description of his wife's unusual character and piety. But the most poignant part, and the most revelatory of his marriage, were his concluding words: "Although it is customary to ask forgiveness from a deceased at his funeral, I will not do so now. This is because we lived our years together in total peace, without either of us ever having in the least hurt one another. I have nothing for which to ask my wife forgiveness."

One wonders how many people there are who could make the same statement.

Although a *tzaddik's* home is full of peace, *Shalom Bayis* is not his exclusive portion. Dedicated work toward the same goals by any couple will produce the same results.

The Third Catalyst

We love, says the Vilna Gaon, because we recognize noble qualities in someone.[2] This is the third catalyst of love (after pleasure, and assistance in achieving one's objectives). But man's egotism makes such recognition hard to come by. We spend too much of our lives fantasizing about how beautiful, intelligent, and important we are while convincing ourselves how ugly, unintelligent, and unimportant others are. Our jealousy makes it difficult for us to acknowledge that another person possesses a superior quality which we lack. How, then, can we overcome these blinders?

One approach is by becoming honest enough to overcome our sense of superiority. But this is a difficult task, because honesty does not come naturally to humans, especially where their prestige is at stake. An easier way is to feel so identified with another person that his success becomes one's own. Just as we do not begrudge ourselves, so do we not begrudge those with whom we are identified. As the Sages say, "Man is jealous of everyone except his child and his student."[3] Anyone with whom we feel a strong sense of identity would also be excepted.

It also becomes easy to recognize the good qualities in another person if that person is someone whom we already love. In other words, whenever one of the other catalysts of love is put into operation, it becomes easier for this one to work as well. This is because all love creates some degree of identity with the beloved. (The Hebrew word for love, אהבה, has the numerical equivalent of אחד, "one," symbolizing the fact that we become one with the object of our love.) Thus, once a person permits himself to feel a sense of gratitude to his wife for all the benefits she bestows upon him (which causes love, as above), he will feel increasingly identified with her and increasingly able to see her good qualities. For this catalyst, as well, gratitude is a vital ingredient.

The Role of Giving

There is another very important way of getting ourselves to identify with others and of activating this all-important catalyst of love. This is by learning to give of ourselves to the person whom we desire to love.

Rav Eliyahu Dessler notes a remarkable truth: we tend to love those to whom we have given more than those from whom we have received. A mother loves her child more than the child loves her mother, and the reason is because the mother gives her entire life over to her child while the child consciously gives very little to her.[4] How is this to be understood?

The act of giving to another person creates a sense of identity with that person: one feels that one's own self exists in him. A mother sees herself in her child because of the amount of her life she has invested in him, and she therefore loves her child just as she loves herself. In contrast, the child, because he has not invested anything in his mother, has no such feeling.

Every mother is convinced that her child has special qualities. These are not necessarily imagined qualities; but because she identifies with her child, she notices aspects in him which no one else can see. Similarly, once we identify with someone it is not difficult to notice all his admirable traits — and to love him for them. We suddenly become aware of qualities of kindness, intelligence, devotion, and so forth, which we failed to recognize previously.

A woman once approached me with a request to help her raise some money for her son. He was, she told me, an outstanding boy who honored his parents, who would go out of his way to do favors for others, who was, in short, a model son. Why did he need money? The woman was quick to explain. He needed a lawyer to defend himself for something which was not his fault, and if he did not get a good lawyer, he could spend years in jail.

The trouble began while he was selling watermelons at a busy intersection, and someone else began selling watermelons at the same corner. They began to argue and the other person pushed him. The son was understandably upset by this. He took his watermelon knife and stabbed the man. Actually, she said, he only scratched him, but for unknown reasons the wounded man died. Her son, the lady explained, did have one fault, and this was that he became too upset over injustice. Because of this fault her son was now in trouble.

Perhaps only a mother can find merit in a murderer, but anyone who feels love for another will inescapably find admirable aspects to his character — aspects which he never before knew existed. The challenge is to overcome the barrier which prevents us from noticing them. We can best achieve this awareness by giving of ourselves to that person.

The sense of identity — and love — produced by giving is increased if the giving entails pain and sacrifice. The greater the giver's suffering, the greater the sense of his own self existing within the recipient.

This might well be the secret behind God's plan in making a mother undergo labor pains when she gives birth. Her suffering is a vital element in her love for her child. In fact, all parents love their children to the degree that they have suffered for them. Often, parents of chronically ill children love them more than many parents love their normal children. This results from the enormous amount of self-denial and suffering which is involved in raising a sick child. As they see their sacrifice manifested in their child, they identify with — and therefore love — him more.

The relationship between suffering and love is reflected in an interesting practice recorded in the Talmud. When a cow endangered its calf by refusing to nurse it, the technique used to revive the cow's maternal instinct was to pour salt into her genital tract, thereby producing a burning sensation. When the cow would feel the pain, it would be reminded of the birth of its young; its maternal instinct would be triggered, and it would begin feeding it.[5] The wisdom which lies behind this is that the maternal instinct is a function of the mother's pain.

Since a sense of identity fosters love, every marriage requires the development of a habit of giving — especially giving which involves self-denial. Generally, this is not too difficult for a wife: her days are usually filled with making life more pleasant for her husband and children, and her life is full of giving. But it is much easier for husbands to become "takers."

It should be noted that besides impeding the development of love, refusing to give will make one increasingly unable to concern himself with other people's needs. This undermines the very purpose of marriage and hastens its collapse.

To make his marriage a success, therefore, a husband should actively seek out ways to make his wife's life more pleasant. The Torah obligates us to spend time thinking about what one can do for our fellow man.[6] The obligation to one's wife is even greater. One should set aside time religiously, whether daily or weekly, for determining what benefits one can render to his wife. It goes without saying that when an opportunity presents itself to act in this manner, one should seize it. One's very marriage can depend upon this.

The Final Stage

We also love, the Vilna Gaon says, for no reason other than that someone loves us. That someone loves us because we must have activated in him one of the catalysts of love. When we sense this, we love him in return.

For one to be able to respond to love in this manner, it is necessary to believe that the other person really loves him. Various people have different degrees of difficulty in believing that someone else can genuinely care for them. Especially in a marriage, this is a very harmful character trait which one should work on and neutralize by making a "leap of faith" and forcing himself to trust his spouse even before he has sound evidence for doing so. For only if one learns to trust a spouse's love can it be possible to respond to his/her love.

On the other hand, it is equally harmful to a marriage to do nothing in the way of expressing affection for a spouse and to rely instead on his/her capacity to trust without reason. On the contrary, we should be doing everything in our capacity to get across the idea that we care about him/her. Words alone are often not enough to express these feelings with full genuineness. What is needed is demonstration by action.

How is this done? Loving means that we are willing to devote ourselves to our beloved's welfare without expecting any personal gain in return. Thus, if we wish to transmit a message that we care for someone, we must show that we are willing to act for his benefit even where we do not stand to benefit or gain recognition by this.

A young man I know, whose wife had particular problems in trusting his love for her, used the following tactic very profitably. Whenever he sensed that he left her in a sad mood, he would place notes in spots where his wife was bound to find them — in cupboards, in closets and in the mailbox — with short messages like: "Cheer up; you have a husband who always thinks of you"; "Smile"; "Your loving husband will soon be back"; and so forth. The thoughtfulness which lay behind these notes, the display of genuine concern for her feelings, helped allay her feelings of mistrust.

It goes without saying that single acts are insufficient for this. One has to be consistent in his demonstrations of love.

As we have said, overcoming the barrier of mistrust fosters the reciprocal love which is the natural response to being loved. But this is not the end of the process. Reciprocal love engenders reciprocal love. As a consequence, the original love is continuously deepened by a spiral of love which is set into motion.

According to the Vilna Gaon, this sort of love represents love in its highest form,[7] and is the love referred to in the Mishna as "love independent of a cause."[8] All other loves, caused by the catalysts of benefits received or of recognition of noble qualities, cease to exist when the cause of the catalyst disappears, such as when the benefits end or the noble qualities change. Love based on a response to another's love is love beyond reason and cannot be terminated by any new situation — as long as the sensation exists that one is still beloved.

This type of love makes it possible for husband and wife to develop the close sense of identity with each other which means a successful marriage. When this stage is reached, the peace of the bird reigns between them, and marriage moves toward it highest level, the level where marriage is described by the prophet Malachi as, "For she is the wife of your covenant."[9]

NOTES TO CHAPTER THIRTEEN

1. Chapter 11: *Fostering Love.*
2. Vilna Gaon, *Commentary to Shir HaShirim 5:2.*
3. *Sanhedrin 105b.*
4. R. Eliyahu Dessler, *Michtav MeEliyahu,* Vol. 1, p. 36 ff.
5. *Shabbos 128b.*
6. Rabbeynu Yonah, *Shaarey Teshuvah* Sec.III, par. 5.
7. Vilna Gaon, *Commentary to Shir HaShirim, ib.*
8. *Avos 5, 16.*   9. *Malachi 2:14.*

EPILOGUE

This book attempts to trace the development of a successful marital relationship according to the principles of the Torah. A successful marriage begins with the peace of the river, grows into the peace of the kettle and finally develops into the peace of the bird.

It begins with two people making a commitment to each other by their marriage.

It develops by their training themselves to fulfil each other's physical and emotional needs; by learning to appreciate the good which they give to each other; by concentrating on giving to each other rather than taking.

The process reaches its fruition with the closest relationship that can exist between any two beings. This is the relationship whose potential God built into man's very creation and which makes it possible for man to reach the goals for which he was brought into this world. The road leading from beginning to successful end is paved by man's and woman's willingness to overcome their selfishness.

In marriage, like in all other areas of living, shortsighted self-interest is man's greatest enemy. Man deludes himself into believing that by exploiting marriage for his immediate benefit he will gain in the long run. However, the reality is that this path inevitably leads to endless misery and unhappiness. The surest thing about marriage is that if one trains himself to crack through the shell of his selfishness, to concern himself with his wife's needs, and to be grateful and giving, his life will be filled with constant joy and happiness.

At every Jewish wedding ceremony, we hear a prayer that God make the newly married couple as happy as He made the first man and woman happy in the Garden of Eden. In that blessing, the first couple, Adam and Chava, are called *"re'im ha-ahuvim"* (beloved friends). These two words describe the two major purposes for which marriage was created: 1) that man and wife help each other *("re'im")*; and 2) that they love each other *("ha-ahuvim")*. With this blessing, we pray at every wedding that the newly married couple will achieve the level of happiness achieved by their forebears in the Garden of Eden.

Adam and Chavah were so happy because they were beloved friends to the highest degree. And the reason they were beloved friends was that they lived before their sin diminished their humanity and tranformed them into egotistical and self-centered beings. In the selfless state which man and woman enjoyed before they chose to transgress God's will, they were able to enjoy the full degree of happiness which marriage was designed to achieve.

When we pray that we be permitted to reach this stage, we are really praying that we be granted the wisdom to control our selfish instincts and to become humans in the full sense of the word. To the extent husband and wife successfully respond to the mission which God places upon them, they will merit becoming the *re'im ha-ahuvim*, those ideal — and idyllic — beloved friends who represent mankind in its perfect state.

תושלב״ע
בהנלי״כ ולאאע״י

GLOSSARY

anav — a humble person

baal mussar — an exponent of Torah ethics

beys midrash — study hall for Torah learning

bochur — an unmarried student

Chafetz Chayim — Rabbi Yisroel Meir HaKohen, d. 5693 (1933), the greatest sage of his times

chessed — kindness

Erev Shabbos — Friday morning and afternoon

esrog — the citron fruit, used during the Sukkos festival

frumkeit — piety

Halacha — Jewish law

Halachic — pertaining to Jewish law

kollel — post-graduate Rabbinic school for married men

matzos — unleavened bread eaten during Passover

mida kenegged mida — reward paid measure for measure

mikveh — bath for ritual immersion

mitzvah (pl. -vos) — a Torah commandment

Moshe Rabeynu — Moses

mussar — Torah ethics

nidah — a woman in her menstrual state

Rambam — Maimonides, the greatest codifier of Jewish law in history

Shabbos — the Sabbath day

Shalom Bayis — marital peace

Sheva Berachos — parties held during the first seven days of marriage

shul — synagogue

sukkah — booths for the Sukkos festival

Sukkos — the Tabernacles Festival

tzaddik (pl. -im) — a completely righteous person

yetzer hora — the evil inclination in a person

Yom Kippur — the Day of Atonement

zuz — a coin of Talmudic times